10-MINUTE IDEAS
FOR EARLY YEARS

Outdoor play

Sandy Green

■ **Quick activities for any time of the day**

■ **Links to Early Le** ... **saving photocopiables**

Credits

Author
Sandy Green

Editor
Sally Gray

Assistant Editor
Jennifer Shiels

Series Designer
Anna Oliwa

Designer
Andrea Lewis

Cover Illustration
Craig Cameron/Art
Collection

Illustrations
Bethan Matthews/
Sylvie Poggio
Artists Agency

Text © 2004
© 2004 Scholastic Ltd

Designed using Adobe InDesign

Published by Scholastic Ltd
Villiers House
Clarendon Avenue
Leamington Spa
Warwickshire
CV32 5PR

www.scholastic.co.uk

Printed by Bell & Bain

2 3 4 5 6 7 8 9   4 5 6 7 8 9 0 1 2 3

British Library Cataloguing-in-Publication Data
A catalogue record for this book is available from the British Library.

ISBN 0-439-97115-2

Contents

Contents

Physical development

Creative development

Photocopiables

Introduction

This book provides a range of new and fresh approaches to short outdoor play activities. As well as being quick to undertake, each activity is quick to set up – with many needing no specific props or preparation. As well as standing in their own right, as planned educational activities, all the activities can be used to fill a few spare minutes, when a little unexpected time arises – as it often does! Many of the activities can be varied according to the environment – the season, outdoor play area, garden and so on, and most can be extended if time allows.

Planning the environment

Finding the right approach to the outdoor play area is an important starting point for your planning. The easiest way is to think of it in the same way as you think of the indoor environment. The outdoor environment should be aesthetically appealing to the children, with an appropriate layout and relevant resources to meet the aims that you are hoping to achieve.

Advice and guidance on making the most of the outdoor environment can be acquired from the national school grounds charity Learning through Landscapes (LTL). They can be contacted at schoolgrounds-uk@ltl.org.uk

Cross-curricular learning

Outdoor play has naturally close links to the Foundation Stage's Early Learning Goals for Physical development and Knowledge and understanding of the world. It should be remembered, however, that it offers scope for all the Areas of Learning and brings a great deal to the overall package of education that young children receive. The activities in this book show how easily the Areas of Learning interrelate and how most ideas give opportunities for cross-curricular learning. It is important to view the outdoor area as an extension of the indoor environment, rather than simply as the outdoor

'slot' in the timetable or daily plan. This offers greater scope for planned ideas and creativity, and encourages children to use opportunities in the fresh air as a matter of course, approaching them with interest and enthusiasm.

How to use this book

The ten-minute ideas included here cover a broad and even spread of the Early Learning Goals across the six Areas of Learning in the Foundation Stage curriculum. The intended outcomes of each activity identify both the Early Learning Goal and a relevant Stepping Stone that can support it. A group size has been suggested for each idea, but many of these can be adjusted according to the numbers of both children and adults within the setting.

Although a suggested Stepping Stone and Early Learning Goal have been given for each activity, readers will see how well many of the activities cross

over into other curriculum areas, or aspects of curriculum areas. For example, 'Making a splash' on page 17 illustrates how a Communication, language and literacy led activity provides scope for Physical development skills, with clear links to the area of Knowledge and understanding of the world. Other examples include the Mathematical development activity, 'Five happy squirrels' (page 27) which offers opportunities for Creative development as well as opportunities to use fine and gross motor (or Physical development) skills. Many of the activities automatically support Personal, social and emotional development, either as individuals or in co-operation with others – examples include 'Working together' page 14, 'Jumping frogs' page 37 and 'Traffic jams' page 53.

Home links

Home links have been suggested, encouraging the inclusion of parents in the learning process. Sometimes, as in 'Rangoli patterns' on page 16 there may be a linked sheet for parents to help their child complete at home. There may also be a suggestion for parents to hold a specific discussion with their child at home such as in 'Our own special rules', on page 13.

Details of well-known books related to some of the activities make excellent additional information for parents, helping to add further links to the activities and also keeping them in touch with their child's progress and developing interests.

Photocopiable pages

At the end of the book you will find a time-saving selection of photocopiable pages. Each photocopiable page is directly linked to an activity, and these links are clearly indicated. Many can also be used on their own, either as support materials for other activities, as activities in their own right, or as a home/setting links. Some of the action rhymes that have been provided are original, and others are based on well-known tunes.

A majority of the photocopiable pages in this book would lend themselves to assessment, helping to provide evidence of a child's level of understanding or achievement.

Assessment

Opportunities for assessment are always important, and early years staff will identify opportunities that fit in with their current plans and are suited to the needs of the children in their own settings. As assessment opportunities are mostly found by observing children during activities, the ideas within this book give opportunities for early years practitioners to both involve themselves with children directly – enabling opportunities for close observation, and also to supervise activities at a distance – allowing observation of how children interact with each other, respond to direction, and initiate actions for themselves.

Multicultural links

Whenever possible, links to culture should be included in planning. The involvement of parents (and other family members) in bringing ideas and artefacts linked to their cultural heritage to the setting, should be both welcomed and promoted.

Personal, social and emotional development

The activities in this chapter encourage children to be independent and initiate interaction with others, to approach new experiences with confidence and be sensitive to the needs, views and feelings of other people while in different social situations.

Find the minibeasts

What you need
Copy of the 'Minibeast hunt' photocopiable sheet on page 67 for each child; pencils; photographs or information books showing minibeasts.

What to do
Ask the children if they know what a minibeast is. Where might they find one? Show them some pictures as examples.

Now explain to the children that they are going to go out into the outdoor play area to look for some different minibeasts. Give each child a copy of the photocopiable sheet and a pencil. Do they know the names of the minibeasts on the sheet? When you are certain that the children know which minibeasts they are looking for, encourage them to wander around on their own or with a friend to see how many they can find.

Remind the children to tick the boxes on the sheet only when they have actually seen that particular minibeast. Encourage the children to tell each other when they have found one, and to take responsibility in showing each other where it is, or where it disappeared. It is important that the children understand that they are to observe, but must never disturb the minibeasts.

Support and extension
Give younger children suggestions of where to look for the minibeasts to get them started. Carefully collect one or two minibeasts to enable older children to observe them more closely, but ensure that after a short time you place them back where you found them.

Further ideas
■ Build a wormery in an old fish tank or a large plastic jar, using layers of soil and sand. Help the children to notice how the soil and sand gradually mixes.
■ Carefully collect minibeasts and provide magnifying glasses and microscopes to help the children to observe them in more detail.
■ Read *The Bad-tempered Ladybird* by Eric Carle (Puffin Books) and *The Very Hungry Caterpillar* by Eric Carle (Hamish Hamilton).

What is missing?

What you need
Variety of garden items such as pebble, twig, plant, flower pot, flower, leaf, gardening glove, snail shell, bird feeder, hand trowel, watering can and packet of seeds; large cloth; copy of the 'Memory game' photocopiable sheet on page 68 for each child.

Preparation
Set the items out on a bench, table or on the ground. Cover with the cloth.

What to do
Invite the children to join you outside, asking them to sit to one side of the covered items. Explain that you will be playing a memory game.

Show the children all of the items under the cover and explain that they need to look at them very carefully, and try to remember what they see. Talk to the children about each item individually and what they are used for.

Cover up the items and ask the children to collectively try to remember all of the things. Uncover them and see if they remembered them all.

Next, cover the items up again, and take one item away, without the children seeing. When you remove the cover, challenge the children to identify what is missing. Repeat the activity as often as you like, depending on the level of enthusiasm and concentration!

Support and extension
Give younger children copies of the 'Memory game' as a prompt and let them work in pairs. Take away more than one item at a time for older children or put one back that had just been removed. Encourage the children to suggest other items from around the outdoor play area that could be included.

Further ideas
■ Make a 'Garden centre' role-play area outside, and let the children buy and sell items, such as the objects from the activity.
■ Provide clean plant pots and seed trays for filling and emptying in the sandpit or water tray.
■ Use leaves and pebbles for sorting and classifying.

Who will play with me?

What you need
Just the children.

What to do
Start the activity by asking the children, 'Who likes to skip?'; 'Who likes to run and jump around?' and so on. Emphasise how lovely it is that so many of them like to do the same things.

Tell the children that they will be going outside and that you would like them to think about the games they usually play. Explain that you want to make sure that everyone has someone special to play with. Start this process by encouraging the first child to say, for example, 'I like skipping. Who would like to skip with me?'. Continue this until every child has joined up with at least one other person. This process works particularly well when there are new children in the setting, or when you are aware that a particular child seems isolated or unable to initiate play with others.

Let the children enjoy carrying out their chosen activity outdoors for ten minutes. Remember, children do not usually mean to be unkind and leave others on their own, they often simply do not notice.

Support and extension
Remind younger children of games they have particularly enjoyed before. Encourage older children to think what it might be like to have no one to play with.

Further ideas
■ Talk to the children about what kindness means, and ask them to tell you about a time when they have been kind to somebody.
■ Play a circle game, singing, 'Who will be my friend today, friend today, friend today; who will be my friend today – who will come and play?'. Encourage one child to be in the middle, then to select a friend to skip with them while

the whole group sings the song again. Each child that joins brings another friend into the middle until all are joining in!
■ Read books about friendship and/or being lonely. Examples include, *The Gotcha Smile* by Rita Phillips Mitchell and Alex Ayliffe (Orchard Books), and *The Rainbow Fish* by Marcus Pfister (North-South Books).

LEARNING OBJECTIVES
STEPPING STONE
Have a sense of belonging.

EARLY LEARNING GOAL
Have a developing awareness of their own needs, views and feelings and be sensitive to the needs, views and feelings of others.

GROUP SIZE
Whole group.

HOME LINKS
Encourage parents to talk to their children about being kind and including others in their play.

Personal, social and emotional development

What should we wear?

LEARNING OBJECTIVES

STEPPING STONE
Initiate interactions with other people.

EARLY LEARNING GOAL
Have a developing awareness of their own needs, views and feelings and be sensitive to the needs, views and feelings of others.

GROUP SIZE
Six to eight children.

What you need
Selection of clothing suitable for different types of weather; clothes basket; pictures depicting weather across a range of seasons.

Preparation
It is helpful to have a discussion about weather and the seasons in advance of the activity.

What to do
Sit outside with the children and discuss what sort of weather it is today and what sort of (appropriate) clothing they are wearing. Briefly remind the children about the need for wearing warmer clothing when it is cold, and about protective clothing for sunny days.

Show the children the weather pictures before turning them face down. Explain that you will ask them, in turn, to pick a card, choose a friend and then suggest some clothes to wear to suit the weather on their card. For example, if they pick a rainy picture they may suggest that their friend wears a raincoat. Their friend must then try to find the item from the clothes basket, put it on and walk or skip around the circle, returning to where they were sitting. They then select a picture and choose a friend, continuing the process until the clothing, and/or pictures have all been used. Repeat the game if all the children did not get a turn.

Support and extension
Suggest that younger children choose the person next to them as their friend. Encourage older children to make a link to a specific outing or journey. For example, 'Ishmal is going to town today – it is raining, so he needs to wear a raincoat'.

HOME LINKS
Suggest to parents that they encourage their children to think about what clothes they need to put on, by considering the weather.

Further ideas
■ Sing songs such as 'Doctor Foster went to Gloucester' (Traditional) and talk about what he needed to be wearing.
■ Provide pictures of different people at work and talk about their different clothing needs. For example, fishermen, lifeboat crews, fruit pickers in summer and so on.
■ Provide piles of clothing for the children to sort by their suitability for different types of weather.

I would like to show you

What you need
Your outdoor play area.

What to do
This is a very simple activity in which children are encouraged to form pairs and share with each other what it is they particularly like about the outdoor play area. Explain to the children that they might like something because of how it looks, how it feels, what it does, what they are able to do with it and so on. Remind them that somebody else may choose the same 'object of interest' as them, but their reason for choosing it may be different, because we all like different things for different reasons.

Take the group outside and help them to divide themselves up, ensuring that no one is left on their own. Ask them to think for a moment about where they will each take their friend and then help them to decide what they will look at first. Once this has been established, send each pair off, giving them time to share their thoughts with each other.

Call all of the children back together as a large group and encourage each pair to tell the others what they had been discussing or looking at. Tell the children that they can either give a description of the object, or they can provide the group with clues. The main point of the activity is to help the children to develop the skills to interact and share.

Support and extension
Encourage younger children to choose who they will work with. Ask older children to explain something about their chosen item or place to the whole group.

Further ideas
■ Play 'I spy', linked to objects or places outside.
■ Have a mobile 'Show and tell' in which the children take the whole group to see what they particularly like outside, saying why they like it.
■ Describe outside places or objects for the children to guess.
■ Provide some visual images of common outdoors objects and places, and encourage the children to share their thoughts about each one.

LEARNING OBJECTIVES
STEPPING STONE
Seek out others to share experiences.

EARLY LEARNING GOAL
Form good relationships with adults and peers.

GROUP SIZE
Whole group in pairs.

HOME LINKS
Encourage the children to describe objects and places that they like around their home for their parents to guess.

Personal, social and emotional development

What will we need?

What you need
Reasonably large sand-pit; different sand tools such as spades, scoops and palette knives.

Preparation
Ensure that the sand in the sand-pit is clean and not too dry.

What to do
Start by taking the children outside and reminding them about the importance of handling sand safely.

Explain that they are each going to make a sandpit model home for their families to live in. Tell the children that they will need to think about the needs of each member of their family and how they will provide for them in the sand home. Give examples, such as a baby needs a cot, grandma may need to sleep downstairs (and so on).

This activity will help the children to understand that everybody has differing needs, linked to their age, ability, culture and preferences.

Provide the children with the sand tools and talk to them about what they are building and why, throughout the activity. Encourage them to share and to ask each other about what they are doing. Make sure that they each respect each other's space and models. Praise the children for helping each other and talk to them about their own family routines and cultures.

Support and extension
Remind younger children of their family members and their likely needs. Try giving older children a specific theme, such as, 'It is Christmas', 'It is Holi' and so on.

Further ideas
- Build a place for 'special' items of interest in the outdoor area.
- Talk to the children about the importance of respecting their own cultural beliefs and those of others.
- Talk to the children about Holi (a Hindu festival) and build a 'bonfire' of items from around the outside area. Dance around it in the Hindu tradition (Holi usually occurs in March).

Our own special rules

What you need
Pen; paper.

What to do
Talk briefly about general safety issues and then take them as a group into the outdoor play area.

Explain to the children that they need to think about safety as they look around the play area. Tell them that you would like their help to make a set of rules to ensure that everyone can play happily and safely whenever they are outside. Give them some examples, such as, 'Play with children who are on their own', 'Do not climb on the fence' and so on.

Send the children off to 'look and think', asking them to come and give you their suggestions when they think of them. Write all their ideas down, explaining to the children that all the suggestions will be discussed at circle (or a similar) time.

Use the children's ideas as the basis for a discussion as soon as you can, while the activity is fresh in the children's minds.

Support and extension
Give younger children some additional suggestions in the form of questions. For example, 'How can we ensure that everyone plays safely in the sand?'. Encourage older children to write all of their ideas down.

Further ideas
■ Provide pictures of hazards, such as an open gate in a play park. Ask the children to explain what the hazard is.
■ Provide pictures of litter and talk to the children about the dangers of leaving it around – to birds and animals as well as humans.
■ Make 'Be careful', ' Play nicely', 'Don't run' signs (and so on) and position them outside in appropriate places.
■ Mark out a roadway and practise crossing the road.
■ Provide a range of visual 'hazard' signs such as irritant, toxic or flammable and talk to the children about them.

Working together

What you need
Old bath towel for each group; balls; beanbags; plastic bottles (some empty, some filled with sand).

Preparation
Lay the towels in a line on the ground outside, with a range of balls and skittles near to each one.

What to do
Explain to the children that they are going to work together in small groups to move all the items from one of the piles on the ground to the far side of the play area by carefully putting the objects on the towels and carrying them. Explain that they can touch the items to put them on the towel but must not touch them during the 'journey' unless they fall off. Encourage the children to think about how to keep the towel balanced, move together and co-operate when any changes in direction are needed, or when someone needs to stop completely.

Place the children into groups of six with one child at each corner of the towel and two on each of the long sides. When they are ready, ask them to walk carefully together across the play area, without dropping any of the items. Afterwards, talk about the difficulties they had.

Support and extension
Let younger children move the items one at a time. Challenge older children to see who can get the most items safely across in the quickest time (without stopping to pick up any that fall).

Further ideas
■ Try the activity using much smaller or larger objects and pieces of material. How does this alter the activity?
■ Place a range of balls on to a towel held up high by four children. Who can knock the balls off from underneath?
■ Place a ball on a towel and encourage the children to gently roll it from end to end, or side to side without letting it fall.

Planting the bulbs

What you need
Copies of 'Pot planting' photocopiable sheet on page 69 for each child; enough bulbs, pots and trowels for each child; soil; water; dustpan and brush; old sheet (optional).

Preparation
Ensure that all items are laid out on the sheet outside. Talk through the planting process with the children, demonstrating it yourself and using the photocopied page as a guide. Please note that many bulbs are poisonous and care must be taken to ensure that the children do not place them in their mouths, and that they wash their hands after handling them. If working with young children take care not to leave bulbs lying around.

What to do
Explain to the children that they are now going to plant some bulbs themselves. Show them the prepared items. Ask the children which items they recognise and name any other items for them.

Show them the photocopiable sheet, explaining that the order on the sheet will help them to carry out the planting. Encourage them to follow the illustrations, helping each other if necessary.

Encourage the children to ask questions about the activity during the process, rather than waiting for adult directions.

Support and extension
Provide younger children with a selection of pictures showing how the bulbs will look like when they have grown. Ask older children to think about what the bulbs will need when they are growing.

Further ideas
■ Provide information books on growing and plants, for the children to look at and share with you.
■ Let the children plant beans, cress and carrot tops indoors and watch them grow.
■ Provide old trays for the children to make a miniature garden, using soil, moss and pebbles, together with mustard and cress seeds.
■ Plant a bed of bulbs in the outdoor play area, and let the children take responsibility for weeding and watering in dry weather.

LEARNING OBJECTIVES
STEPPING STONE
Operate independently within the environment and show confidence in linking up with others for support and guidance.

EARLY LEARNING GOAL
Select and use activities and resources independently.

GROUP SIZE
Six to eight children.

Take care!
Many bulbs are poisonous.

HOME LINKS
Encourage parents to allow their children to grow carrot or parsnip tops on kitchen paper on an old saucer – lovely ferns are produced if they are kept moist. Also, encourage them to read stories such as *The Enormous Turnip* (Ladybird books).

Rangoli patterns

What you need
Examples of rangoli patterns; chalks; safety mirrors.

Preparation
Lightly draw an outline of squares on the ground in chalk, outside a doorway (make each square approximately 20cm across). Ensure that this is not an emergency exit.

What to do
Take the children outside and start the activity by talking to them about rangoli patterns. Explain that these patterns are set out by Hindu people (often in coloured rice) at the entrance to their homes as a welcome to their visitors during the festival Divali. The patterns (which mostly consist of squares, lines and triangles) are usually symmetrical (the patterns look the same from all directions) and this is one of the main features of rangoli.

Show the children the examples that you have prepared and explain to them how they can extend patterns 'symmetrically' by holding a mirror against one design and looking at both the pattern and the mirror image of the pattern at the same time. Give each child some chalks and encourage them to design a pattern in a chalked square on the ground, in the style of the examples you prepared for them. Provide safety mirrors for them to see how the design would look if reversed.

Encourage the children to try and reverse their design in chalk. As each child completes their squared-pattern, invite another child from the group to join in the activity, adding more and more designs until the whole 'welcome mat' is completely finished.

Support and extension
Explain clearly to younger children what is meant by the word 'symmetry' – giving them plenty of different examples (such as left and right hands, left and right feet and so on). Encourage older children to copy a prepared symmetrical design, repeating the (reversed) design across the mat.

Further ideas
■ Provide mirrors for children to experiment further with reversed images and symmetry.
■ Talk about Divali and what it means to Hindu people (and some Sikh people as well).
■ Let the children make rangoli patterns on pieces of square card and mount them as a wall display.

LEARNING OBJECTIVES

STEPPING STONE
Have an awareness of, and show interest and enjoyment in, cultural and religious differences.

EARLY LEARNING GOAL
Understand that people have different needs, views, cultures and beliefs, that need to be treated with respect.

GROUP SIZE
Four children at a time.

HOME LINKS
Send home copies of 'Rangoli drawings' photocopiable sheet on page 70 and encourage parents to help their child draw reversed images at home too.

Communication, language and literacy

While taking part in these ideas, children will learn to respond to simple instructions, listen to stories with increasing attention and recall, use their imagination, build up their vocabulary and hear and say initial sounds in words.

Making a splash

What you need
Medium-sized balls (enough for one between every pair of children); PE hoops; skipping ropes; playground chalk.

What to do
Begin the activity by explaining to the children that they are going to pretend to splash each other in imaginary areas of water outside. Invite the children to join you outside and explain to them that the PE hoops will be puddles, the skipping ropes will be lakes, and with the playground chalk you will make an ocean on the ground.

Ask the children to think about the sounds that are made if a ball is thrown into a puddle, a lake or an ocean. Help them to develop a range of descriptive words for these actions (splash, splosh, plop, splat, swoosh and so on).

Next, place the hoops and the ropes (in uneven 'lake' shapes) around the outdoor area, and draw a large ocean with the chalk. Pair the children up, giving each of them a ball. Ask them to move around the play area passing the ball to each other by bouncing it through the puddles, lakes and so on. Each time they bounce it in an area of water, they must call out a sound to describe it splashing. Encourage them to use as many words as possible.

Support and extension
Remind younger children of the words that they can choose from. Encourage older children to make up words when they run out of words they know.

Further ideas
■ Encourage the use of descriptive language when the children are at the water tray (such as pour, drip, run, gush).
■ Talk about local areas of water (ponds, lakes, rivers and so on) and ask who has been to see them. Remind them of the importance of keeping safe.
■ Paint ripple patterns and display them.
■ Sing songs such as 'Doctor Foster went to Gloucester' (Traditional).

LEARNING OBJECTIVES
STEPPING STONE
Build up vocabulary that reflects the breadth of their experiences.

EARLY LEARNING GOAL
Extend their vocabulary, exploring the meanings and sounds of new words.

GROUP SIZE
Whole group.

HOME LINKS
Ask parents to talk to their children about how they use water at home, and its importance to their lives.

Simon says move like a...

What you need
Just the children.

What to do
Make sure that the children are familiar with the traditional game, 'Simon says'. Invite them to join you outside and explain to them that they are going to play a new version of the game.

Explain that instead of showing them an action (as in the traditional 'Simon says' game), you will describe the action for them, and they must interpret it for themselves. Explain that in between each action you will call out, 'Simon says be still' and explain that this is where they must stop and listen for the next instruction.

Now give them some examples, accompanied by appropriate actions such as, 'Spin like a helicopter' or 'Float like a magic carpet'. Remind them again that they must listen for each action to end and the next to begin.

Keep the focus of the actions to one outdoors theme, such as transport – examples you could use include, 'Zoom like a rocket, fly like an aeroplane'; or creatures – 'Fly like a butterfly, swoop like a bird, hover like a dragonfly'.

Support and extension
Provide younger children with several example actions before you start the activity. Encourage older children to interpret the actions of words such as 'exciting', or prehistoric creatures – for example, 'Run like a Stegosaurus' or 'Fly like a pterodactyl'.

Further ideas
■ Introduce 'Simon says' into everyday routines. For example, 'Simon says line up at the door'.
■ Talk to the children at circle time about why it is important to listen.
■ Read stories such as *Don't Forget the Bacon!* by Pat Hutchins (Red Fox) and discuss listening and concentrating.

Run to the gate if...

What you need
Just the children.

What to do
Start by talking to the children about the similarities they notice between themselves and other children in the group. Give them examples, such as having a ponytail, having blue eyes or wearing a red jumper.

Explain that you are going to take them outside and play a game in which you are going to give them a set of instructions, such as, 'Run to the gate if you are wearing red'; 'Hop to the tree if you have a ponytail'. Tell the children that they must try to decide if the instruction applies to them or not. If the instruction does apply, they need to do what you have asked. If it does not apply, they need to wait for another instruction.

Once the game has started, keep providing new categories until all the children have moved to one specific place. You will need to re-word the instruction so that children who have already moved stay put! For example, after the first go you will need to say, 'Move, or stay at the gate if you have…'. The game can begin again if time allows.

Support and extension
Simplify the activity for younger children by asking them to simply 'stand up', or 'sit down' rather than 'run to the gate' – the game ending when everyone is sitting down (or standing up). Challenge older children by adding extra details, such as, 'Run to the gate if you have more than three buttons'.

Further ideas
■ Provide a range of pictures (such as trees, flowers and leaves) for the children to sort and classify.
■ Focus on a specific feature, such as the colour of one child's jumper and ask the children to identify as many items outside that match the colour.
■ Identify an object in your mind and let the children try to guess what it is by listening to the clues you give them. For example, if you were thinking of a buttercup, your clues might include, 'It is the same colour as the sun' or 'It grows in the grass' and so on.

LEARNING OBJECTIVES
STEPPING STONE
Respond to simple instructions.

EARLY LEARNING GOAL
Sustain attentive listening, responding to what they have heard by relevant comments, questions or actions.

GROUP SIZE
Whole group.

HOME LINKS
Ask parents to help their children to note similarities between family members, for example, who has the same hair colour, eye colour and hair type.

Listen and run

**LEARNING
OBJECTIVES**
STEPPING STONE
Respond to simple
instructions.

**EARLY LEARNING
GOAL**
Sustain attentive
listening, responding
to what they have
heard by relevant
comments, questions
or actions.

GROUP SIZE
Whole group (in
groups of no more
than eight children).

What you need
Just the children.

What to do
Start the activity by taking the children outside and asking them to listen very carefully. Encourage the children to practise 'whispering voices' before the game begins.

In a whisper, explain the rules of the game to the children. Tell them that they will take it in turns to whisper one of the actions, 'hop, skip or jump' to another child. The child that is whispered to must perform the action, landing opposite another child who they, in turn, will whisper to.

Ask the children to stand in a circle and start the game by whispering 'hop' to one of them. That child must hop across the circle to the person roughly opposite him, whisper an action to him or her and then sit down in the space that he or she leaves. The process continues until all the children have had a turn and are sitting down.

Support and extension
Divide large groups, or groups of younger children into smaller units. Bear in mind that some younger children may have difficulty hopping. Do not provide suggestions of actions for older children, and challenge them to try and make each action they whisper different to the ones already used.

Further ideas
■ Show the children simple hand signs and try to communicate by only using these signs.
■ Ask the children when they have noticed people whispering and why they think this happens (such as in churches, mosques, hospitals and libraries).
■ Perform action rhymes without the singing – who can be the first to identify the rhyme? Good examples would be traditional songs such as 'Wind the Bobbin Up' or 'Head, Shoulders, Knees and Toes'.

HOME LINKS
Encourage parents
to help their children
to develop listening
skills by talking very
quietly to them
or by whispering
instructions to them.

Walking through the garden

What you need
Just the children.

What to do
Take the children out into the outdoor play area. Ask them to look around carefully and to comment on anything that they notice. Discuss all the things that the children can see.

Explain to the children that you are all going to walk slowly around the outdoor area together, looking closely at things. Tell them that they are going to help you recite a story, and that they will each, in turn (when tapped on the shoulder), add a detail to the story.

Start the story by saying, 'I am walking through the garden (playground...) and on my way I have seen a hedge (path, wall, fence, stone...)'. Tap a child on the shoulder – they must repeat what has already been said and then add on an observation of their own. For example, the story may continue as, 'I am walking through the garden, and on my way I have seen a hedge and a pebble'. That child must then tap another child on the shoulder and the game continues, for example, 'I am walking through the garden, and on my way I have seen a hedge and a pebble, and a drainpipe...'.

The aim of this activity is to make the list as long as possible, including every child into the story at least once.

Support and extension
Help the younger children by recounting the previous items along with them. Introduce sounds for older children, for example, birds singing, cars hooting, dogs barking and so on.

Further ideas
■ Play games at circle time such as 'I went to the shops and in my basket I bought...'.
■ Read simple story books such as *Don't Forget The Bacon!* by Pat Hutchins (Red Fox).
■ Sing songs that contain cumulative rhymes, such as the traditional Christmas song, 'The Twelve Days of Christmas'.

The insect's journey

What you need
Just the children.

What to do
Introduce this activity by taking the children outside and asking them who they think might live in the outdoor play area.

Once you have established that this might include a range of insects, encourage the children to think about where they might be in the garden and how they may travel around it. Encourage the children to consider the ways that insects move, such as crawling, flying, going over, across, underneath and through things.

Now explain to the children that you are all going to make up a story about one of the insects. Agree on an insect that you would like to have at the centre of the story. Start the story for them. For example, 'The caterpillar was on the gate, he wriggled slowly along to the edge and then he …'. Invite a child to continue the story, for example, '…curled up and rolled off the edge, landing on the ground, where he…'. The story builds up as each child adds the next part of the insect's journey. Encourage the children to use a variety of directions and positions in their contribution to the story.

Support and extension
Remind younger children how different insects move to help them understand where they could and could not manage to go. Encourage older children to demonstrate insect movements to each other and to the younger children.

Further ideas
■ Sing the rhyme 'Gordon the gardener' on the photocopiable sheet on page 71 and carry out all the actions.
■ Encourage the children to move like various insects.
■ Invite the children to help you to make a display of the insect's journey on a roll of wallpaper or lining paper. Ask each child to draw their part of the insect's journey onto the paper.

LEARNING OBJECTIVES
STEPPING STONE
Build up vocabulary that reflects the breadth of their experiences.

EARLY LEARNING GOAL
Extend their vocabulary, exploring the meanings and sounds of new words.

GROUP SIZE
Whole group.

HOME LINKS
Encourage parents to help their children to think of ways to describe their journey to and from the group. For example, 'Along the road, through the arch' or 'Down the hill' and so on. Send home copies of 'Gordon the gardener' photocopiable sheet on page 71 and encourage parents to say the rhyme with their children at home.

What am I?

What you need
Just the children.

What to do
Talk to the children about the activity before you take them outside. Explain to them that they are going to play a game in which they need to describe something for the rest of the group to guess.

Help the children to understand the game by giving them an example, using an item indoors. For example, 'It is brown. We rest on it when we are drawing. It is made from a tree. What is it?'. Once the children have guessed 'table', talk to them about the clues you gave them. Explain that you gave a clue about the colour, a clue about what it is used for and a clue about what it is made from. Suggest that the children might use similar clues when it is their turn to describe something. You may need to remind each child as they have their turn.

Group the children together in small groups of up to four and take them outside. Give them a short time to look around and decide on an object to describe. Now ask them to think of some clues for the object.

Invite a group at a time to present their clues to the rest of the children. Encourage each child in the group to present a clue, in turn. Suggest that the children give just one clue at a time, to see how many clues are needed for the other children to guess the object.

Support and extension
Help younger children to choose their clues. Challenge older children by suggesting objects that they are familiar with but are not visible to them at that time.

Further ideas
■ Provide puzzles of single item pictures that the children can try to identify before the whole picture is put together.
■ Suggest that the children draw or paint different objects from outside, then display them. Encourage the rest of the group to identify and say what the pictures show.
■ Draw a picture on the ground in chalk. How quickly can the children identify what it is?

LEARNING OBJECTIVES
STEPPING STONE
Begin to use talk to pretend imaginary situations.

EARLY LEARNING GOAL
Use language to imagine and recreate roles and experiences.

GROUP SIZE
Whole group.

HOME LINKS
Suggest to parents that they play 'What am I?' with their children at home, focusing on objects in the home or the garden.

What am I doing?

What you need
Just the children.

What to do
Start the activity by taking the children outside and asking them to imagine that they are in a big garden. Can they think of all the actions that are carried out by people working in the garden? Examples include digging, raking, planting, sweeping up, mowing the lawn, cutting a hedge, watering plants and so on.

Now explain to the children that they are going to pretend to carry out a gardening action like this for everyone else to guess. Tell them that they can give verbal clues to help if they want to. For example, 'My mummy does this at home', or, 'This is very hard work'. With a large group, divide the children into groups of six to eight.

Let each child carry out an 'action' for the others in their group to identify. As each child takes their turn, encourage the other children to look at the action carefully and to ask questions to find out more.

Support and extension
Suggest actions for the younger children to demonstrate. Encourage older children to demonstrate the actions without speaking. Invite the other children to ask lots of questions, to which the child demonstrating may only answer yes or no.

Further ideas
■ Encourage the children to use their body to make shadows against a wall in the sunshine. Can they make their shadows do some gardening actions?
■ Talk to the children about the way their bodies move. Use vocabulary such as bending, twisting, stretching, reaching, pulling, pushing and so on.
■ Draw a chalk 'tightrope' and see who can walk along it. Can the children control their bodies?
■ Teach the children how to play a simple playground game such as hopscotch. Help them to co-ordinate their actions.

'A' is for ant

What you need
Board or puzzle with 'lift-out' alphabet letters.

What to do
Invite the children to come outside with you and tell them that they are going to play a letter sound game.

Give each child a letter from the alphabet puzzle. Ask them to say the name of the letter and the sound that it makes. Next, ask them to look around the outdoor play area and tell you what they can see that begins with that sound. Give them some examples to make the game clear, such as, 'A is the letter sound for ant'; 'B is the letter sound for buttercup'; 'C is the letter sound for caterpillar' and so on.

Explain to the children that each time they have identified something that begins with the letter sound, they must come and tell you. If they are correct they may keep the letter before choosing another one. Continue the game until all the (viable) letters have been chosen.

Invite the children to take turns to show the rest of the group their collected letters. Encourage them to remember all of the objects they found that go with each of their letter sounds.

Support and extension
Write the letter shape for younger children and ask them to match it to the correct 'lift out' letter. Encourage older children to show younger children the correct letter if they are unable to identify it for themselves.

Further ideas
■ Ask the children to think of actions or positions they can demonstrate, for as many letters as possible, such as, 'A is for asleep'; 'B is for bending';' C is for climbing' and so on.
■ Provide dried alphabet pasta shapes for sorting out or for making an alphabet collage picture.
■ Provide solid three-dimensional letter shapes for the children to print with.
■ Look at alphabet books and talk about the items that start with each letter.

LEARNING OBJECTIVES
STEPPING STONE
Hear and say the initial sound in words and know which letters represent some of the sounds.

EARLY LEARNING GOAL
Link sounds to letters, naming and sounding the letters of the alphabet.

GROUP SIZE
Eight children.

HOME LINKS
Encourage parents to use letter sounds with their children. Suggest a 'letter of the week' for them to focus on, helping their child to identify as many items around the home that begin with that particular letter sound.

Bees make honey

What you need
Card in various colours; bright yellow card; clear tape; scissors; small box.

Preparation
Cut flower shapes from the coloured card (approximately 15cm across), enough for one per child. Add circles of clear tape to the backs of each flower to enable them to stick to the children's clothing. Cut hexagon shapes from the bright yellow card (approximately 20cm across).

What to do
Tell the children that they are going to go outside and play a game called 'Bees make honey'.

Find out what the children know about bees and how they make honey. Talk to them about the process. Now organise the children into a large circle, place your box in the middle and choose the first 'bee' to stand next to it.

← 15cm (6") →
diameter

Give each child a yellow hexagon to hold. Explain to the children that the yellow hexagons are the nectar that the bees collect from the flowers to make honey. Ask the children to join in with you as you chant, 'Busy bee, busy bee, to make your honey, come to me'. The 'bee' then buzzes over to a 'flower', to collect a hexagon of nectar. The 'bee' places it in the box and then joins the circle, letting the other child become the 'bee'. The game should continue until all the children have been a 'bee' and all the yellow hexagons are put into the box.

Support and extension
Show the children pictures of flowers and point out where the bees gather the nectar from. Let the children lay out the hexagons of nectar to make a honeycomb effect on the ground.

Further ideas
■ Make honey sandwiches and have them at snack-time. Ensure that no children have allergies to honey.
■ Provide the group with yellow and black paint, and encourage the children to paint bumble bees.
■ Create wax pictures using beeswax candles, overwashed with thin paint.

Mathematical development

This chapter suggests a range of ideas to help children recognise numerals 1 to 9 and start to count beyond 10, begin to relate addition and subtraction, place items into order by weight, match shapes by recognising similarities and orientation and use everyday words to describe position.

Five happy squirrels

What you need
Pictures of squirrels in different poses, such as showing their bushy tails, how they hold food in their front claws, how they curl around and how they hang from branches of trees or bird tables to reach bird feeders; the song 'Five happy squirrels in a tree' on the photocopiable sheet on page 72.

What to do
Start by showing the pictures to the children, explaining how squirrels move about and feed. Tell them that squirrels often take food that is put out for the birds. Talk about how squirrels store nuts and berries to eat during the winter, and ask the children to think about why they need to do this.

If possible, play out this activity under an oak tree – taking the children outside and grouping them around it – explaining that this is the sort of tree that squirrels particularly like because of the acorns. Otherwise, any tree or space will suffice.

Introduce the action song, 'Five happy squirrels in an old oak tree', agreeing which children will be the five squirrels this time. Sing and perform as the traditional 'Five currant buns in a baker's shop' rhyme – starting with five children as the squirrels and gradually reducing the numbers, until there are no squirrels left. Repeat the song, giving other children a chance to be squirrels.

Support and extension
Support younger children as they learn to count down from five. Encourage older children to say the next number in the counting down sequence without your help.

Further ideas
■ Provide pictures for sequencing, such as, acorn, oak tree, squirrel, nuts.
■ Use oak leaves for making leaf rubbings.
■ Encourage children to look out for squirrels and to make a chart to show how many have been observed.

LEARNING OBJECTIVES
STEPPING STONE
Say with confidence the number that is one more than a given number.

EARLY LEARNING GOAL
In practical activities and discussion begin to use the vocabulary involved in adding and subtracting.

GROUP SIZE
Whole group.

HOME LINKS
Encourage children to look out for squirrels near to their homes, and suggest to parents that they read stories such as *The Tale of Squirrel Nutkin* by Beatrix Potter (Frederick Warne).

How many children?

LEARNING OBJECTIVES
STEPPING STONE
Recognise numerals 1 to 5, then 1 to 9.

EARLY LEARNING GOAL
Recognise numerals 1 to 9.

GROUP SIZE
Six (or ten) children.

What you need
A5-sized pieces of card showing the numerals 1 to 9.

What to do
Invite the children to come outside with you and ask them to stand in a line. Explain to them that they are going to be counting children and adding numbers of children together.

Choose one child to start the activity by 'making a gap' in the line of children, dividing them up into two smaller lines. Ask the child to count how many children are now on each side of the line. Emphasise the outcome – for example, 'Two children and three children adds up to five children'. Ask all the children to check the amounts and say the number sentence together.

Now ask another child to select the correct number cards to represent the children on each side, for example, three and two, and also the total number – five. Make sure that each child has a turn at counting and selecting the dividing point.

It is important to repeat the activity to reinforce the concept, using outdoor objects such as plastic plant pots, hoops and pebbles every time.

Support and extension
Younger children will need help to make a different gap to the previous child. Support their counting efforts by counting out loud with them, pointing at each child as they count. Encourage older children to make the division and to count the numbers of children out loud on their own.

Further ideas
■ Laminate the cards and place small pebbles onto each one to encourage individual understanding of numbers, such as two pebbles on number 2, four on number 4 and so on. Count them with the children.
■ Hang a short clothes line on the wall or fence. Place a dividing mark in the middle. Let the children peg socks or other small items onto each side, to consolidate understanding of adding one and two, two and two, and so on.
■ Provide activities that encourage adding on one more, such as threading leaves, daisies and buttercups.

HOME LINKS
Ask parents to help their children to add groups of items together using household objects such as spoons, cups and toothbrushes.

How many pebbles?

What you need
Small plastic cup for each child; pebbles that the children can collect from around the outdoor play area (put these out yourself in advance if necessary).

What to do
Invite the children to join you outside and give each of them an identical container. Explain that they need to go and fill up their container with pebbles from around the play area.

After a while, invite the children to sit down with you and ask them to guess how many pebbles they have collected in their container. Write their answers down for them. Next, help each child, in turn, to count out their pebbles.

As each child's pebbles are counted, ask the next child questions such as, 'Do you think your pebbles are larger, smaller or the same sort of size?' or, 'Is your container as full, more full, or less full?'. Remind them how many the previous child had collected and ask them once again how many they think they have in their container. Encourage them to think, 'I might have more because…' or, 'I might have less because…' and so on.

Repeat the questions for each child in the group and compare all the different amounts. Now let the children scoop up fresh amounts of pebbles to guess, count and compare.

Support and extension
Help younger children to count their pebbles. Encourage older children to make their comparisons and estimations both before they tip them out of the pot, and also when they are spread on the ground.

Further ideas
■ Suggest other opportunities for estimating outdoors, such as asking, 'Which stick do you think is the longest?' before the children actually hold them against each other.
■ Explore issues such as, 'Is the biggest always the heaviest?' and let the children experiment with different objects, such as comparing a stone with a clod of earth, or a piece of wood with a square of turf and so on.
■ Provide weighing scales to help children identify which items are a similar weight, and which are the heaviest or lightest.

LEARNING OBJECTIVES
STEPPING STONE
Begin to count beyond 10.

EARLY LEARNING GOAL
Use developing mathematical ideas and methods to solve practical problems.

GROUP SIZE
Four to six children.

HOME LINKS
Ask parents to encourage their child to estimate, for example, 'How many steps to the next lamp-post? How many biscuits in the packet' and so on.

How many butterflies now?

LEARNING OBJECTIVES
STEPPING STONE
Say with confidence the number that is one more than a given number.

EARLY LEARNING GOAL
In practical activities and discussion begin to use the vocabulary for adding and subtracting.

GROUP SIZE
Eight children.

What you need
A4-sized medium-weight cardboard sheet for each child; scissors; access to a fence or wall; double-sided tape or Blu-Tack; crayons.

Preparation
Cut out a simple butterfly shape from the card for each child. Ask the children to colour them in bright colours in advance of the activity. Attach circles of double-sided tape (or Blu-Tack) to the reverse side of each butterfly.

What to do
Explain to the children that they are going to use their butterflies for a counting game. Take them outside and show them the fence (or wall) you have chosen to use. Position two or three butterflies onto the fence as a starting point.

Ask the children how many butterflies they can count and then ask them, in turn, to either add one butterfly or take away one butterfly – each time asking the question, 'How many butterflies are there now?'. As the children become more confident with their use of number, increase the numbers of butterflies that you use.

If the weather is good, leave the butterflies on the fence, and occasionally change the number, to encourage the children to count them regularly, identifying increases or decreases in their numbers on their own initiative.

HOME LINKS
Ask parents to help their children to add on and take way in situations at home. For example, 'I have taken one biscuit, now there are two left', or 'If Daddy eats this apple, there will be three left in the fruit bowl'.

Support and extension
Encourage younger children to count from number 'one' each time, and challenge older children to add on or take away two butterflies, or to try to add on numbers in their head.

Further ideas
■ Play games and sing rhymes that add on or take away, such as the song 'Ten Green Bottles' (Traditional).
■ Provide a range of natural items for the children to count, such as acorns, conkers and leaves.

Pebbles in the pond

What you need
Two PE hoops for each child; large container (such as an ice-cream tub); a selection of pebbles or small stones.

What to do
Invite the children outside and explain that they are going to pretend that the PE hoops are ponds. Tell them that they will be using the ponds for some counting practice.

Ask the children to collect some pebbles or small stones and put them in the container. Now give each child some pebbles from the container (vary the amounts to suit the children's different abilities). Ask each child to count the pebbles you have given them, telling you how many they have.

Next, allocate two hoops to each child and tell the children to place some of their pebbles into each of their 'ponds'. Then ask them to count the pebbles in each pond in turn, helping them to develop their understanding of understanding of numbers as they see that three pebbles and two pebbles make the same (five) as the five pebbles they started with, and so on.

Encourage the children to repeat the activity many times, each time altering the numbers of pebbles in the ponds.

Support and extension
Give full adult support to younger children as they divide up and count their pebbles. Encourage older children to use a higher number of pebbles, and to both add on and take away, continuing to move pebbles from pond to pond.

■■■■■■■■■■■■■■

Further ideas
■ Emphasise the use of number and number division when sharing out resources between the children.
■ Provide activities that involve the children having to share or count out objects, such as beanbags, balls, hoops and so on.
■ Consolidate the use of number in practical situations such as meal or snack times.
For example, 'Can I have two more children at this table please?' or 'How many more children need a drink?' and so on.

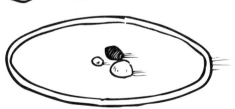

LEARNING OBJECTIVES
STEPPING STONE
Find the total number of items in two groups by counting all of them.

EARLY LEARNING GOAL
Begin to relate addition to combining two groups of objects and subtraction to 'taking away'.

■■■■■■■■■■■

GROUP SIZE
Eight children.

■■■■■■■■■■■

HOME LINKS
Encourage parents to reinforce adding and taking away when shopping with their children, laying the table for dinner and so on. For example, 'We have four spoons. If we give Mummy one, how many will we have left?'.
■■■■■■■■■■

Sand, and more sand

What you need
Range of containers of different heights and diameters (two of each type whenever possible); sand.

Preparation
Set out the range of containers in a suitable place in the outdoor play area. Place the sand nearby.

What to do
Take the children outside and explain to them that you are going to ask them to look carefully at some containers, deciding which could contain the same amount of sand and which might hold more or less.

Start by filling one container with sand. Ask the children to tell you which container they think matches it. Pour the sand from the first container into the container the children have chosen to see if they are correct.

As the children's confidence with the activity grows, fill two different-shaped containers with sand and ask the children if they think they contain the same amount of sand or not. If they think they will be different, ask them which they think will hold the most (or least) sand.

Repeat the game a few times and then question the children about their reasons. For example, 'Why do you think the two containers will hold the same amount of sand?' or 'What makes you think they hold the same amount – is it the shape of the container?' or 'Have you lifted them to feel how much they weigh?' and so on. Help the children to check the outcome each time by pouring the sand from the second container into a container that matches the first container.

Support and extension
Limit the number of containers for younger children. Encourage older children to think of as many ways as they can to describe how they made their judgements, based on height, width, shape and weight.

Further ideas
■ Use water, soil or gravel as alternatives to sand.
■ Provide (sealed) plastic containers of sand for weighing and balancing.
■ Encourage volume and capacity activities in the water tray.
■ Play skittles, using different-shaped (sealed) containers of sand.

Three sides or four?

What you need
Playground chalk; pictures of shapes (square, rectangle, circle, triangle); copies of 'Name the shape' photocopiable sheet on page 73 (optional).

What to do
Explain to the children that they are going to go outside with you to help you make shapes on the ground. What shapes can they think of?

Show them the pictures of the shapes and explain that these are the shapes that you would like the children to try and 'make'. Encourage the group to help you count out loud the number of sides and the number of points that each shape has.

Now ask the children to try and make some of the shapes by standing together in different arrangements. Help them to make a shape at a time – for example, three children positioned into a triangle, four children positioned into a square and so on.

Draw a chalk line between each child and then let the children move away to see how the shapes have been formed. Find extra shapes with the children by using the chalk to make lines from corner to corner to form shapes within shapes, such as four small triangles within a square and so on.

Ask the children to identify the shapes and help them to count how many shapes have been made.

Support and extension
Help younger children to match the pictures you showed them to the shapes on the ground, and help them to count the shapes. Encourage older children to choose the shape and work out how many children will be needed to set it out.

Further ideas
■ Encourage the children to find as many shapes with three or four sides as they can, in and around the outdoor play area.
■ Ask the children which is the largest three- or four-sided object that they can see.
■ Play 'Spot the shape' when out and about with the children. For example, when out shopping (round apples, square loaves, triangles of cheese) or in the street (round wheels, square windows, triangle-shaped roofs).

LEARNING OBJECTIVES
STEPPING STONE
Match some shapes by recognising similarities and orientation.

EARLY LEARNING GOAL
Talk about, recognise, and recreate simple patterns.

GROUP SIZE
Eight children.

HOME LINKS
Give the children a copy of 'Name the shape' photocopiable sheet to take home. Encourage parents to help their children look for shapes around the home.

Sorting out

LEARNING OBJECTIVES

STEPPING STONE
Show curiosity and observation by talking about shapes, how they are the same or why some are different.

EARLY LEARNING GOAL
Talk about, recognise and recreate simple patterns.

GROUP SIZE
Six to eight children.

What you need
Several large PE hoops; range of garden items such as pebbles, twigs, plants, bulbs, packet of seeds, different-sized rocks, flower heads, empty snail shells, sticks for supporting plants, pieces of bark, leaves, watering 'roses' from watering cans.

What to do
Invite the children to accompany you outside and lay out the PE hoops and the garden items in front of them. Be aware that some bulbs are poisonous and make sure that all of the children wash their hands after handling the garden materials.

Check that the children can all see the complete range of items. Talk to the children about the shape of each item in turn, asking them how it compares to the shape of the other items.

Encourage the children to think of ways to sort the materials according to whether they are plants, creatures, natural or man-made objects, as well as by more obvious attributes such as shape and colour. Give them some starting-points by asking questions such as, 'Is it natural or man-made?' or 'Would you use it or grow it?' and so on.

Now challenge the children to sort the selection of items into groups of their own choosing. Let them sort the materials, then ask the children to say what they think is the same about all the items that they have grouped together. How many do they have in each group?

Support and extension
Remind younger children of the properties of the objects throughout the group activity. Encourage older children to find additional items to include from around the outside play area.

HOME LINKS
Explain to parents that the children have been sorting 'by function' and encourage them to continue this at home, sorting items for the kitchen, the bathroom, the garden and so on.

Further ideas
■ Let the children print with suitable items from each 'group' they have made (such as different types of leaves), again discussing similarities and differences between their shapes.
■ Make rubbings of bark and stones. How do they compare?
■ Use pebbles to mark out a snail shell design on the ground. How many different-shaped (or colour) pebbles can they find?

Finding shapes outside

What you need
Examples (or pictures) of 2-D and 3-D shapes (such as rectangle, circle, cube and cylinder); copies of 'Identifying shapes' photocopiable sheet on page 74.

What to do
Invite the children to join you outside and explain to them that they are going to be looking for specific shapes outdoors. Show them the examples you have selected and remind them of the names of each shape, specifically indicating the three-dimensional aspects.

Give each child a copy of 'Identifying shapes' photocopiable (page 74) to help remind them of the shapes they are looking for. Ask the children to look carefully around the play area and identify as many shapes as they can.

Move around the play area with the children, prompting them by asking them questions or making suggestions, such as, 'Does this object remind you of one of the shapes?' and 'How would you describe this object?' or 'Which shape do you think this is like?' and so on.

Support and extension
Remind younger children to keep referring to the sheet of illustrations and if appropriate, concentrate on just two or three chosen shapes. Encourage older children to remember the names of the shapes themselves.

Further ideas
■ Provide the children with a cloth-bag containing a range of 3-D objects for them to identify by touch.
■ Collect small 3-D boxes such as stock-cube boxes, triangular cheese boxes, tubes and so on. Encourage the children to sort and classify them for a table-top display.
■ Use shape terminology in everyday activities by making statements such as, 'What a big circle we are sitting in today', or by asking questions such as, 'Who would like to do the puzzles at the square table?' or ' Who would like to print at the rectangle-shaped table?' and so on.

LEARNING OBJECTIVES
STEPPING STONE
Begin to talk about the shapes of everyday objects.

EARLY LEARNING GOAL
Use language such as 'circle' or 'bigger' to describe the shape and size of solids and flat shapes.

GROUP SIZE
Eight children.

HOME LINKS
Ask parents to provide a range of three-dimensional boxes for your collection. Encourage the children to show their boxes at circle time, describing and naming the shape if possible. Let the children take home copies of the 'Identifying shapes' photocopiable sheet to use with their parents.

Mathematical development

Up the hill, down the road

LEARNING OBJECTIVES

STEPPING STONE
Describe a simple journey.

EARLY LEARNING GOAL
Use everyday words to describe position.

GROUP SIZE
Up to 12 children.

What you need
Just the children.

What to do
Go into the outdoor play area with the children and stand together in a circle. Tell them that you are going to go on an imaginary journey together.

Explain that you will start a story and that you would like them to take it in turns to add a bit to it. Say that it will be about a journey and ask the children to choose someone as the focus of the journey (such as a man, child, dog or horse). What sort of places will their character travel to? Encourage them to think about journeys they have been on themselves to give them some ideas. Provide suggestions for words to use, such as 'around', 'along', 'over', 'between', 'across', 'next to' and so on.

Start the story by saying, for example, 'Mr Jones walked up the hill,' (invite the children to walk on the spot). The next person then adds to the story, '...and round the corner,' (everyone pretends to turn a corner). The story develops in linked stages according to the children's choices (past the trees, round the pond, over the railway bridge, through the gates, behind the factory, and so on). Help them to come up with relevant actions as the story evolves, making use of the landscape in your outdoor area wherever possible.

Support and extension
Use gestures to help younger children to get started. Suggest to older children that they could let the journey take them to an exotic place, drawing on their imagination even further afield – 'Mr Jones landed on the moon and...', and so on.

Further ideas
■ Record the story and listen to it again later on.
■ Encourage the children to describe the whole journey, repeating what has been said already and adding another bit.
■ Tell the children the story of a journey you have taken, and encourage them to 'act it out' on the spot.

HOME LINKS
Encourage parents to help their children 'think through' and describe a walk or journey they know well, such as the walk to school, to Granny's house or to the shops.

Knowledge and understanding of the world

This chapter suggests ideas to enable children to describe and remember simple features of objects and events, to look closely at similarities, differences, patterns and change and show an interest in why events happen and question how things work.

Jumping frogs

What you need
Copy of 'Frog fun' photocopiable sheet on page 75 for each child; A4-sized sheet of medium weight card for each child; playground chalk, scissors.

Preparation
Copy the frog template on page 75 for each child and ideally let the children colour or paint them at an earlier time. Cut out the frog shapes. Use the playground chalk to draw a pond on the ground outside.

What to do
Give each child their frog shape and a sheet of card. Explain to them that you are going to play a game in which they will be making their frogs jump.

Take the children outside and ask them to show you how they think frogs jump. Encourage them to use their back legs to spring forwards, just like real frogs do! Give them the cut-out frogs and point out the back legs.

Using a piece of stiff card, demonstrate to the children how waving the card swiftly behind the frogs can make them 'leap' forward. Show them the chalk pond shape and explain that the game is to get all the frogs into the 'pond'.

Support and extension
Give particular help to younger children who may find the action difficult to start with. Encourage older children to help them, too. They may children might also like to make the activity into a race, seeing which frog reaches the pond safely first.

Further ideas
■ Sing the action rhyme 'Five Little Speckled Frogs' (Traditional).
■ Play 'Follow the frog' around the outdoor play area with each child 'jumping' behind the frog in front of them.
■ Find out more about other creatures, from newts to ducks, that might live in a pond.
■ Look out for frog spawn if you have a real pond and observe it developing/changing into tadpoles and frogs over time.

Growing the bread

What you need
Pictures of a loaf of bread and/or wheat or corn; deep tray of soil (half-filled); some extra soil in another container; metal spoon or small trowel; seeds for planting (if possible, use wheat or corn); a large jug of water or a watering can; a bench or low table; copies of 'There was a gardener long ago' photocopiable sheet on page 76.

Preparation
Prepare the tray of soil in advance and identify a bench or low table that the children will be able to rest on whilst they plant their seeds. Photocopy the rhyme from page 76.

What to do
Show the children the pictures and help them to name what is shown. Explain that wheat and corn are used to make flour and that this in turn is used to make bread. Ask the children what else they can think of that is made with flour. If necessary, give them examples such as pasta, biscuits and cake.

Take the children outside and talk through the process you want them to follow – sprinkling the seeds onto the tray of soil, covering them with more soil and then watering carefully. Clear up any mess together.

Now follow the actions and rhyme on page 76 with the children. As you progress through the rhyme, introduce the actions for each verse to the children and encourage them all to join in.

Support and extension
Younger children will probably need some help to sprinkle the seeds and pour the water carefully. Older children can be given additional responsibilities such as carrying the water and the soil, or collecting appropriate items needed in order for them to plant the seeds.

Further ideas
■ Make sandwiches and have a picnic outside.
■ Make a display of different types of breads from around the world.
■ Once the seeds have started to sprout, encourage the children to measure and monitor them.

Investigating leaves

What you need
Plenty of fallen leaves in the outdoor area; large shallow container such as an old baby bath.

Preparation
Ensure that all the leaves in the area are safe for the children to handle, and remind the children not to pick the leaves from trees, plants or bushes.

What to do
Take the children out into the outdoor play area and explain that you want them to collect as many different types of leaves as they can find. This activity is best suited to the autumn months when there are naturally more fallen leaves available.

Provide the children with the large container and ask them to place all the leaves they can find inside it. Challenge them to find a different leaf each time. Once they have collected several leaves, start to examine them with the children. Encourage them to compare the types of leaf, and discuss together what is similar and what is different about each kind. Ask them questions such as, 'Which leaf is the longest? Which is the broadest? Which is the darkest?'. Which leaves do the children think have come from the same type of tree or bush? Ask them to explain why they think that.

Support and extension
Help younger children to match the leaves. This will help them to make comparisons more easily. Introduce new words such as 'sap' and 'veins' to extend older children's knowledge and vocabulary.

Further ideas
■ Use PE hoops to group the leaves by one (or two) features. Which hoop has the most leaves? Do some leaves fit into more than one category?
■ Make leaf rubbings using paper and crayons.
■ On a windy day, see who can catch leaves in a pond net.
■ Challenge the children to see who can pick up the most leaves in a set amount of time, using large objects such as two tennis rackets, or small objects such as tweezers or sausage-tongs.

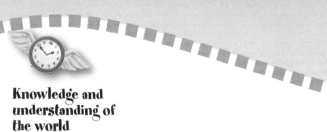

What is it made of?

LEARNING OBJECTIVES

STEPPING STONE
Show an interest in why things happen and how things work.

EARLY LEARNING GOAL
Ask questions about why things happen and how things work.

GROUP SIZE
Whole group.

What you need
Just the children.

What to do
Explain to the children that you are going to help them to find out more about some of the everyday objects that they see around your outdoor play area, such as the climbing frame, the storage shed and the bird feeder.

Take the children outside and group them near to your first selected object. Encourage them to ask you lots of questions about the object and see who else can answer the questions before doing so yourself.

Alternatively, ask the children some simple questions, for example, 'What is it made of?', 'What is it for?' or 'What does it do?', 'How does it work?' or 'What holds it together?' and 'How strong do you think it is?'.

Now invite the children to touch and explore the objects in question. Does it help them to answer any of the questions? Have they changed their minds about any of the previous answers that were given?

Support and extension
Give a range of suggested answers to younger children as prompts to help them. Invite older children to work in small groups or pairs, and encourage them to pose questions for each other.

HOME LINKS
Ask parents to help their children to identify objects around the home made of a particular material, such as wood, metal or stone.

Further ideas
■ Play an adapted version of 'I spy'. For example, 'I spy with my little eye something wooden beginning with…'.
■ Make some trails around your play area with objects all made from the same material, such as wood or metal. Challenge the children to move around the trails, using their knowledge of materials to lead them to the next link. Suggest that older children make up trails for each other to follow.
■ Provide a range of information books about different sorts of materials and what they are used for.

Invisible painting

What you need
Empty paint pot for each child or pair of children (ideally provide paint pots with non-spill lids); clean paintbrush for each child.

Preparation
Half fill each paint pot with cold water.

What to do
Explain to the children that they are going to go outside and paint with invisible paint. Encourage the children to guess what the paint is made from. Give them clues, such as, 'Everyone uses it everyday' or 'We could not live without it' and so on.

Take the children outside to the outdoor play area and give each child a brush. Ensure they have access to a pot of 'invisible paint'. Tell them that they may paint something in the play area. What will they choose first? Offer suggestions such as painting the leaves on the bushes to make them shiny, covering a paving stone or painting a row of bricks.

Talk to the children about how the 'paint' changes the colour of whatever it covers. Discuss where it goes to and why some surfaces take longer to dry than others.

Support and extension
Paint alongside younger children to encourage discussion about the way that water makes objects change colour (temporarily). Give older children washing-up bottles of water for them to 'spray paint' with. Ensure that there is careful adult supervision.

Further ideas
■ Paint a river across the play area and play 'Can I cross the river please?' by lining up all the children (except one) on one side of the 'river', with the other child on the opposite side. The children call, 'Can we cross the river please?' and the child on the other side says, 'Yes, if you are wearing a red/green/yellow jumper' and so on. The game continues until all the children have crossed.

■ Encourage the children to paint pictures on the ground for the rest of the group to identify.

■ Paint a trail of splodges for others to follow.

■ Water the plants in the outdoor play area.

Planning a route

LEARNING OBJECTIVES

STEPPING STONE
Perform simple functions on ICT apparatus.

EARLY LEARNING GOAL
Find out about and identify the uses of everyday technology and use information and communication technology and programmable toys to support their learning.

GROUP SIZE
Up to six children.

What you need
At least one programmable toy (one between two children is ideal); playground chalk; sheets of A1 paper; pen.

Preparation
Check that the children know how to operate the programmable toy. Talk to them about how the toy moves and whether it can make sharp turns or gentle curves, whether it goes fast or at a steady pace.

What to do
Ask the children to bring the programmable toy into the outdoor play area and explain to them that they are going to plan a route for it to travel along. Tell them that they will then be guiding it along this planned route.

Encourage the children to decide on a purpose for the route, for example, the toy needs to find its way back to the toy box, or the boat needs to get to the harbour.

Suggest to the children that they begin by drawing a simple route onto a sheet of paper. When they are happy with their chosen route, let them replicate it on the ground with the chalk. Follow this up by programming and then activating the toy to follow the route.

Discuss with the children how easy or difficult they find the activity. Is it hard to follow a planned route? Encourage the children to take turns in route-planning and activating, ensuring that everyone is involved.

Support and extension
Plan a very simple route for younger children to follow with your help. Older children may like to try and include some small humps within their route if the suitable surfaces are available.

HOME LINKS
Ask parents to talk to their children about 'controlled' vehicles whenever they see them in the streets or on television.

Further ideas
■ Provide dumper trucks and diggers and other 'mechanical' vehicles to use in the sand-pit.
■ Show the children pictures of vehicles that need careful manoeuvring, such as cranes, fork-lift trucks and tractors.
■ Encourage children to bring similar toys from home for a special 'Show and tell' session.

Out and about

What you need
Picnic blanket.

What to do
Invite the children to join you on an imaginary picnic outside in the play area. Ask the children to tell you about any picnics they have been on. Encourage them to talk about where it was, what they had to eat and drink, and what else they did during the picnic. What would they choose to eat now if this was a real picnic?

Help the children to remember other events or experiences in their lives, keeping the focus on those that took place out of doors. As well as special events and unusual activities (such as a trip to the seaside, going to a carnival or attending a wedding), encourage the children to talk about everyday experiences such as walking to the shops or the park, so as to include all the children in the discussion.

Ask the children to explain how they felt on these outdoor activities and why they think they felt like that.

Support and extension
Give younger children confidence by making suggestions to get them started. Encourage older children to try and remember details such as the season, the weather on the day or how old they were when the event took place.

Further ideas
■ Provide photographs of outdoor events to prompt the children.
■ Encourage the children to mime an action indicating an event for the others to guess, for example, paddling in the sea or waving a flag at a street procession.
■ Play 'On the picnic we ate...', with each child adding another yummy item to the list as you continue around the circle.
■ Make paper planes and fly them outside, to represent journeys by air.
■ Create a montage of photographs of family events outdoors and display them around the setting.

LEARNING OBJECTIVES
STEPPING STONE
Remember and talk about significant things that have happened to them.

EARLY LEARNING GOAL
Find out about past and present events in their own lives, and in those of their families and other people they know.

GROUP SIZE
Six to eight children.

HOME LINKS
Ask parents to send in a photograph or an artefact to illustrate a special or favourite event.

Granny's grapes

What you need
Props for the children to use as they act out 'The journey of the grapes': hats for drivers, boat captain and so on; basket for the picker; a hoe for the planter, a shopping bag; plastic grapes.

What to do
Start by holding up the bunch of grapes, and ask if anyone knows where they come from and how they grow. Explain to the children that they were grown outdoors on a vine. Tell them that they are going to act out a story describing how Granny bought her grapes – where she bought them and where they originally come from.

Take the box of props outside and invite the children to join you on the grapes 'journey'. Briefly talk to the children about what each 'person' in the sequence is doing – planting, picking, driving and so on, and allocate different roles to some of the children.

Talk the children through the story. For example, 'The farmer is planting the seeds that will grow into the grapes, the fruit pickers are gathering in the

grapes from their vines, a truck driver collects the grapes and drives them to the harbour, the grapes are loaded onto the boat, the boat captain steers the boat across the sea, when the boat arrives a lorry driver collects the grapes and delivers them to the supermarket, the supermarket staff place the grapes onto the shelf where they are finally bought by Granny'.

Support and extension
Include pictures of vineyards, boats and lorries to help younger children follow the journey. Encourage older children to add their own actions to represent their role in the process.

LEARNING OBJECTIVES
STEPPING STONE
Show an interest in the world in which they live.

EARLY LEARNING GOAL
Observe, find out about and identify features in the place they live and in the natural world.

GROUP SIZE
Whole group.

Further ideas
■ Talk about what the children like about grapes – their taste, colour, shape and so on.
■ Talk about what grapes are used for – wine, fruit juice, dried fruit.
■ Taste different-coloured grapes and make a chart showing who liked which grapes the best.
■ Change the focus of the activity to other fruit and vegetables, such as bananas, yam and spices.

HOME LINKS
Ask parents to talk to their children about where various shopping items might have come from.

Can you find me?

What you need

Five or six clear pictures of 'things' that can be found in (or seen from) the outdoor play area, such as a fence; bird-table, tree, building and climbing frame, suggestions for less obvious items include a herb patch, snail, or specific bush such as holly or lavender.

Preparation

Prepare the pictures you want to include in the activity in advance and laminate them if possible.

What to do

Invite the children to join you outside and explain that you will be dividing them into small groups, and giving them a picture to look at. Tell them that they must help each other to find the item on their group's card. The children must also decide what they like about it and what they would like to know about it.

Give the children a few minutes to do this and then gather all the groups back together. Talk about the pictures. Encourage each child to contribute with either what they like or a question linked to their picture. Whenever possible, let the children answer each other's questions.

Support and extension

Ensure that younger children are given the more easily found pictures. If possible give older children a picture each.

Further ideas

■ Provide every group with an outline plan of the outdoor area for children to mark where they saw the item on their sheet.

■ Help the children to take photographs of items or places in the outdoor area that can be identified by others in the setting, or used in a similar activity.

■ Suggest that the children draw some pictures of objects that they find in their own homes. Let them take the pictures home, suggesting that they challenge their parents or siblings to find and talk about the objects!

LEARNING OBJECTIVES

STEPPING STONE
Comment and ask questions about where they live and the natural world.

EARLY LEARNING GOAL
Find out about their environment, and talk about those features they like and dislike.

GROUP SIZE
Whole group for the discussion; small groups for activity.

HOME LINKS
Explain to parents what the children have been doing, and encourage them to answer the children's questions about objects and artefacts from around the home.

Safari mix up

LEARNING OBJECTIVES
STEPPING STONE
Show an interest in the world in which they live.

EARLY LEARNING GOAL
Observe, find out about and identify features in the place they live and the natural world.

GROUP SIZE
Whole group.

What you need
Pictures or information books showing animals that can be seen on a safari such as elephants, zebras, lions, antelopes and hippos.

What to do
Take the children outside and sit them in a large circle. Talk to them about animals that live in parts of the world where you can travel on 'safari'. Explain what a 'safari' is and tell them that they will each be given the name of an animal that can be seen on 'safari'.

Agree with the children which animal names you will use and then name each child as a specific animal, such as a zebra, lion, antelope, elephant or hippo, ensuring that there are at least two of each type.

Assign the role of caller to one child and give them a special place to sit. Explain that they need to start the game by calling out the name of an animal, such as 'hippo'. Tell the children that when they hear the name of their animal called out they must immediately change places with each other.

The game continues with the child varying the order in which they call the names of the animals, until they finally call out 'safari' and everyone has to change places.

Another child then becomes the caller and the game can begin again.

Support and extension
Remind younger children which animal they are and prompt them when to move. Suggest that older children move around the group in the style of their allocated animal.

Further ideas
■ Play the game using other groups of animals, such as marine life (fictional mermaids, fish, sharks and so on).
■ Let children paint pictures of the animal that they like best.

HOME LINKS
Encourage parents to watch children's wildlife programmes on television with their children. Ask parents to talk to them about the animals they see.

Physical development

This chapter provides ideas for children to experiment with moving confidently and safely, begin to show hand-eye co-ordination, combine and repeat a range of movements, show respect for the personal space of others, whilst being aware of their own space and observe the effects of activity on their bodies.

Wiggle like a worm

What you need
Area of dry grass (or PE mats); plastic bottle; six pictures of different minibeasts such as a worm, spider, grasshopper, snail, caterpillar, ladybird.

Preparation
If using PE mats, place them outside. Laminate the pictures of each minibeast if possible.

What to do
Take the children outside and ask them to name the minibeasts on the pictures you have prepared. Talk to them about how each minibeast moves and let them practise the movements.

Lay out the pictures in a circle and explain that you are now going to spin the bottle in the middle of them. Tell the group that whichever picture the top of the bottle points to when it stops will be the minibeast that they must move like.

After each spin, let the children move for two or three minutes. Talk to them about their movements, and point out any children that are moving imaginatively before bringing them back to the bottle. Repeat the process over and over, trying to 'land' on each picture at some point.

Support and extension
Encourage younger children to all move in the same direction to avoid collisions. Challenge older children by spinning the bottle while they are still moving, encouraging them to change their actions swiftly and frequently.

Further ideas
■ In groups, encourage the children to move as minibeasts in races, such as spiders versus snails, worms versus grasshoppers. Which minibeasts are fastest?
■ Spin the bottle and encourage the children to try and find the selected minibeast in the outdoor play area (not all the pictures will be appropriate for this game).
■ Encourage the children to mime the actions of a minibeast for others to try and identify.

LEARNING OBJECTIVES
STEPPING STONE
Experiment with different ways of moving.

EARLY LEARNING GOAL
Move with confidence, imagination and in safety.

GROUP SIZE
Whole group.

HOME LINKS
Explain to parents that you are currently focusing on movement, linking this to minibeasts. Ask them to continue this at home, asking their children to 'hop to the bathroom', 'crawl into bed' and so on.

Physical development

Follow the squares

LEARNING OBJECTIVES

STEPPING STONE

Go backwards and sideways as well as forwards.

EARLY LEARNING GOAL

Move with confidence, imagination and in safety.

GROUP SIZE

Six to eight children.

What you need

Carpet squares (at least 36).

Preparation

Lay the carpet squares in a linked formation out in the outdoor play area.

What to do

Show the children the laid out carpet squares and explain to them that they are going to use the carpet squares like paving stones. Tell the group that you will be asking them to move around the 'paving stones', one step at a time, in the direction that you choose (forwards, backwards or sideways).

Talk to the children about directions, ensuring that they understand which way to move when you give an instruction.

Now ask each child to choose a 'paving stone' to stand on. Suggest that they space themselves out around the 'pavement'. Give the children clear instructions, such as, 'Take two steps forward, three steps backwards, one step sideways' and so on. If anyone has to step off the carpet squares to complete an instruction, they must sit down and watch.

The activity continues until all the children have run out of carpet squares or until your ten minutes is used up.

Support and extension

Let younger children decide the direction that they will move for themselves, counting as they move. Encourage older children to take turns to call out the directions for the others to follow.

Further ideas

■ With small numbers of children play musical 'squares', in the same way that you would play 'Musical chairs'.

HOME LINKS

Ask parents to emphasise the directions they are moving in when they talk to their children or when they are out together.

■ Use different-coloured carpet squares and spread them out around the outdoor area. Ask the children to skip around until they hear you call out the name of a colour. The children then have to try to sit on a carpet square of that colour.

■ Include PE hoops in the formation, where the children need to 'miss a move' if they have landed on one.

Caterpillars, caterpillars

What you need
Suitable surface for the children to crawl on, such as dry grass or safety playground surface.

What to do
Take the children outside and talk to them about caterpillars, focusing on how they move and how they eventually turn into butterflies. Explain that they are going to play a game called 'Caterpillars, caterpillars', where they will form caterpillar shapes and move together as caterpillars until you tell them to become a butterfly.

Explain that to do this they need to bend forward, one behind the other, in lines of six, lightly resting their hands on the hips of the child in front of them. Tell them that as 'parts' of caterpillars they will need to travel along carefully behind the person in front of them, always ensuring that they are connected. Emphasise that they need to move very slowly, because this is what caterpillars do. Tell the children that you will let them move around for a while as caterpillars, before asking them to stand up and fly around the area as butterflies!

Assemble the lines of caterpillars and explain that the front person is the head of the caterpillar who will choose the direction the caterpillar goes in.

Once the caterpillars are all moving, touch one and call out, '1, 2, 3, 4, 5, this caterpillar is now a butterfly'. The activity continues until all the children have become butterflies.

Support and extension
Provide younger children with a selection of pictures showing caterpillars and butterflies to remind them what they are. Read books such as *The Very Hungry Caterpillar* by Eric Carle (Hamish Hamilton) to older children.

LEARNING OBJECTIVES
STEPPING STONE
Experiment with different ways of moving.

EARLY LEARNING GOAL
Move with confidence, imagination and in safety.

GROUP SIZE
Whole group, in groups of six children.

Further ideas
■ Give children a copy of 'Counting the caterpillars' photocopiable sheet pn page 77 and help them to count the caterpillars. Can they find any real caterpillars around the play area?
■ Use 'on the spot' movements to demonstrate life-cycles or change, such as caterpillar into butterfly, acorn into oak tree, egg into chick.
■ Draw a large butterfly shape on the ground in chalk and let the children decorate its wings with items from around the outdoor play area.
■ Encourage the children to draw a caterpillar or butterfly by copying one they have seen outside.

HOME LINKS
Ask the children to bring in colourful materials from home to make a butterfly collage to put on the wall.

Under, over or in between

What you need
A range of large items outside such as tyres, benches, furniture, outdoor equipment that can be used to form obstacles.

Preparation
Position your selected obstacles appropriately to offer a range of restricted space challenges for the children.

What to do
Start the activity by taking the children outside and talking to them about how much space they take up, if they make themselves as big and wide as they can.

Encourage the group to stand apart from each other and stretch right up, and then out with both arms, turning slowly, without touching anyone else. Next, ask them to try and make themselves as small as they can. Show them how to do this in two ways – by curling up small and low, and by standing up with their arms closely tucked into their sides and their tummies drawn right in.

Talk about the differences in the ways they have made themselves small and explain that they might find this useful in the game you are going to play. Tell them that they will be trying to pass through some obstacles without touching them with any part of their bodies.

Demonstrate how to pass through one of the obstacles, asking the children to watch carefully to see if you touch anything. Now let them take turns to do the same. Gradually reduce the width or height of the same obstacle, making the challenge harder and harder. Encourage the children to watch each other carefully for anybody touching the sides of the obstacle.

Support and extension
Use just one obstacle within a skipping or hopping circuit for younger children. Provide older children with a combination challenge, where the spaces they need to manoeuvre between, alternate between vertical and horizontal.

Further ideas
■ Involve the children in planning and identifying obstacles for each other, under your supervision.
■ Talk to the children about places where people need to fit within narrow gaps, such as turnstiles at football grounds, or where there are low ceilings such as in caves or cellars.

Count the claps

What you need
A range of equipment to create a circuit such as a large storage box, tunnel, bench, PE hoops.

Preparation
Make a circuit from your chosen equipment, ensuring that the circuit will give the children opportunities to move under, over, through and round. Do not include high equipment such as slides or climbing frames, as the excitement of the activity could lead to falls.

What to do
Take the children outside and talk to them about the circuit you have set out for them. Ask them to describe what they can see to you. Do they have any ideas of ways they could move around it?

Now demonstrate some of their ideas as well as your own, explaining each movement as you go. For example, 'I am stepping through this hoop, I am walking along this bench, I am wriggling through this tunnel and climbing over this box'.

Now tell the children that they are each going to take a turn to move around the circuit, one at a time. As each child takes their turn, ask the other children to clap them on their way. Practise clapping together and then encourage the children to count the claps too. How many claps did everyone take?

When everyone has been around once and the children are familiar with the circuit, they could follow each other around it, staggering their start to avoid bumps and collisions.

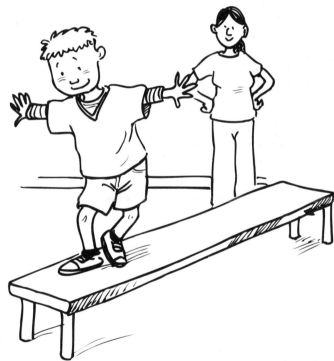

Support and extension
Help younger children to simply clap in time with each other, without counting. Encourage older children to estimate how many claps will be needed to make it round the circuit.

Further ideas
■ Show the children how to use a stopwatch and let them time each other.
■ Set up balancing activities such as children walking along the bench with beanbags on their head.
■ On dry grass or a soft playground surface, lay out a large blanket for children to wriggle under. Who can keep in a straight line?

The moving train

What you need
Spacious, uncluttered area.

What to do
Start the activity by asking the children who has been on a train. Talk to them about how the carriages of a train are linked together and how they travel along, one behind the other, following the same route.

Explain to the children that they are going to come outside with you to be trains, and that they will need to listen carefully to the directions the trains are told to travel in. Tell them that they will need to carefully watch the person (or carriage) that is in front of them, ensuring that they stay together.

Divide the children into trains of six parts and agree who will be the engine on each train. Help the children to think of ways to link up with the carriage in front of them. When everyone is 'secure' and you have ensured that the trains are spaced away from each other to avoid collisions, start all the trains on their journeys.

Give simple instructions in the form of a story, such as, 'The trains are chugging slowly along the track because they are going uphill. As the trains go over the hill they begin to travel faster and faster. The trains are approaching a station and need to slow right down – they are going slower and slower, until they have stopped' (and so on).

As the children begin to get better at moving in synchrony, give more difficult instructions such as rocking sideways, turning corners, reversing into the sidings and so on. At the end of each journey, let another child be the engine and start the activity from the beginning again.

Support and extension
Give visual clues to younger children to help them understand which way to go. Encourage older children to take it in turns to be the person who gives the directions.

Further ideas
■ Provide a range of pictures of trains throughout the ages and discuss with the children the differences between them.
■ Make some flags for 'train guards' to use.

LEARNING OBJECTIVES
STEPPING STONE
Adjust speed or change direction to avoid obstacles.

EARLY LEARNING GOAL
Move with confidence, imagination and in safety.

GROUP SIZE
Whole group, in grouos of six children.

HOME LINKS
Encourage parents to take their children to watch trains passing, and talk about any train journeys they have been on.

Traffic jams

What you need
Just the children.

What to do
Start the activity by talking to the children about vehicles. What are their favourite vehicles? What other vehicles can they tell you about? What do they know about them? Encourage the children to include tractors, road sweepers and diggers in their discussion, as well as cars, lorries, buses, motorbikes, fire-engines and so on.

Now tell the children that they are going to go with you outside, to move around like the vehicle of their choice. Ask them not to tell you what they are going to be and explain that you will be trying to guess from the way that they move. Explain that it is fine for some vehicles to make their movements on the spot (such as cranes, diggers and so on).

Agree with the children which way the road is going to go and encourage them all to move carefully in the same direction. As you correctly guess a vehicle, invite that child to help you guess the next one, until all of the vehicles have been identified.

Support and extension
Give suggestions of vehicles and their actions to younger children. Chalk a 'roundabout' on the ground, and help older children to understand the need for vehicles to stop and give way.

Further ideas
■ Set out a mock zebra crossing and practise crossing the road, emphasising stopping, looking and listening, and crossing with an adult.

■ Play traffic lights by using three sheets of card, one with a red light drawn onto it, one with an amber light and one with a green light. Tell the children to move around the area as their vehicles and hold up the cards as in a traffic light sequence. Ask them to, 'stop', 'go' and 'slow down' to match the appropriate colour cards. This will encourage the children to look and respond to visual instructions.

■ Encourage the children to take turns giving hand signals to direct the traffic.

LEARNING OBJECTIVES
STEPPING STONE
Show respect for other children's personal space when playing among them.

EARLY LEARNING GOAL
Show awareness of space, of themselves and of others.

GROUP SIZE
Whole group.

HOME LINKS
Encourage parents to make a specific focus on teaching their children to cross the road safely.

How does it feel?

LEARNING OBJECTIVES

STEPPING STONE
Observe the effects of activity on their bodies.

EARLY LEARNING GOAL
Recognise the changes that happen to their bodies when they are active.

GROUP SIZE
Whole group.

What you need
Large space, access to a sand-pit (optional), copies of the photocopiable sheet 'Running like a race horse' on page 78.

What to do
Talk to the children about being fit and healthy, and the importance of exercise. Ask them what sorts of exercise (if any) they do, and when they do the most exercise. Explain that they are all going outside to use their bodies by jumping, hopping, marching, running on the spot and so on.

Once outside, encourage the children to 'warm up' their bodies with some gentle bending and stretching. Next, introduce your chosen actions to the children, such as jumping, striding, hopping, bending and stretching, marching up and down, and so on. Encourage the children to follow your instructions and ask them questions such as, 'Do your legs feel any different?' or 'Can you feel your heart beating faster?'. If you have access to a sand-pit, encourage the children to think how different it feels to run on the spot (or

jump) in the sand, compared to on the ground. Gradually introduce different types of steps such as leaping, springing and striding. Remember to emphasise the question, 'How does it make us feel?'.

Now learn the action rhyme 'Running like a race horse' on the photocopiable sheet on page 78. Link the actions you have been practising to the actions that go with the song, and perform the action rhyme together as a group.

Support and extension
Ask younger children specific questions such as, 'How do your legs feel?' or 'Can you feel your heart beating?'. Encourage older children to think what actions could make their legs feel different or how they could make their heart beat faster.

Further ideas
■ Provide the children with beanbags and encourage them to pretend to be weightlifters, showing them how to hold the beanbags correctly.
■ Show the children pictures of athletes and talk to them about the athletes' training and levels of fitness.
■ Play action games such as 'The Grand Old Duke of York', encouraging the children to march around the play area.

HOME LINKS
Ask parents to point out examples of people carrying out healthy activities on television, in magazines, and in real life to their children.

Balance the beanbag

What you need
A container of beanbags, enough for each child.

What to do
Invite the children to join you outside and show them that you can balance a beanbag on your head. What do they think you need to remember when you are doing this – such as you must keep your head still and remember to turn your body carefully.

Ask each child to select a beanbag and stand near to the wall. Encourage them to stand very still while they get it balanced securely on their head. Once they are feeling secure, encourage them to walk slowly across to the other side of the play area, and then to try moving back again more quickly, all the time concentrating on keeping the beanbag balanced.

Once the children have managed to keep it well-balanced on their head, encourage them to try balancing it on other places, such as on their shoulders, in the crook of their arm and on the back of their neck. Remember that careful supervision is always needed when children are moving and balancing, to avoid falls through lack of concentration or over-excitement.

Support and extension
Let younger children balance the beanbags on the palm of their hands instead of their heads. Suggest that they walk to a specific point to put it into a box. Encourage older children to try using less easy items to balance such as balls or quoits, or to walk around obstacles as they balance things.

Further ideas
■ Provide information books showing people from around the world carrying different items in various ways, such as coal miners carrying sacks of coal, hod carriers carrying bricks, African people carrying water containers on their heads and so on.
■ Mark out a short distance for children to walk carrying a full cup of water. Can they manage not to spill any?
■ Have 'egg and spoon' races using hard-boiled eggs or potatoes.

The spider's web

What you need
A hexagon-shaped piece of board or soft wood for each child; nails with largish heads; hammer; wool; scissors; a picture of a spider's web.

Preparation
Hammer the nails into the board in advance to form a spider's web effect.

What to do
Start the activity by taking the children outside and asking them to look for a spider's web. If you do not manage to find one then show them your picture of one. Point out the main features of the web, such as the long linking threads that fan out from the centre.

Talk to the children about what the webs are for and how spiders catch flies and other insects in the sticky threads. Explain to the children that they are going to make spider web designs on the boards. Show them how to wind the wool around the nails, imitating the way a spider spins its web.

Look at the real web or picture again. Tie a length of wool to one nail on each board, and encourage them to weave and wind the wool around the nails. Refer them to the design in the picture to help guide them in making their own design as much like a real web as they can. Encourage them to describe and explain the process as they work.

Support and extension
This activity will help to develop younger children's fine motor skills. They may need some help to get started and will need guidance to create a simple pattern. Let older children use child-sized real tools (under strict adult supervision) to hammer in the nails to make their own spider's web boards. Draw their attention to the importance of handling tools safely.

Further ideas
■ If possible, watch a spider at work, spinning its own web across a gateway or bush.
■ Read younger children books such as *Emily's Legs* by Dick King-Smith (Hodder Wayland) and read stories such as *Charlotte's Web* by E B White (Puffin Books) to older children.
■ Make web designs in damp sand with fingers or sticks.

Creative development

The chapter suggests ideas to enable children to explore colours, textures and shapes, learn how sounds can be changed and use resources to create props to support role-play, encourage play alongside others who are engaged in the same theme and put together a sequence of movements.

Observe and colour

What you need
At least one sheet of paper for each child; clipboards or similar for them to rest on; range of coloured pens, pencils, crayons or chalks.

Preparation
Have a look at what is visible in or beyond your outdoor play area, include flowers, trees, stones, berries, storage sheds, climbing frames, fences, drainpipes and so on. Make a note of the colours represented by the various items.

What to do
Explain to the children that you will be going outside to do some drawings of the things that they can see.

Talk to them about the range of colours they are going to be choosing from, showing and naming each one in turn. Tell them that you would like them to try and choose colours for their drawings that are the same as the objects.

Go outside and talk to the children about what they can see. Help them to focus on objects high up as well as at eye-level. Which items do they think they could draw?

Now give them some examples of how they might choose an object and what colours they might use, such as, 'If I was going to draw the grass, I would choose the green crayon'. Encourage the children to draw at least two items during the ten-minute activity.

Support and extension
Help younger children to match colours by spending some time identifying the colours of the objects before you begin. Help older children to use paints to mix the colours they need.

Further ideas
■ Name items for the children to colour that are not currently visible from the outdoor play area (again matching the colours accurately). For example, daffodils, holly, a robin, blossom and so on.
■ Give children a colour and ask them to make a representation of something that is usually that colour.

LEARNING OBJECTIVES
STEPPING STONE
Choose particular colours to use for a purpose.

EARLY LEARNING GOAL
Explore colour, texture, shape, form and space in two or three dimensions.

GROUP SIZE
Whole group.

HOME LINKS
Encourage the children to bring in a picture they have drawn and coloured correctly, of something from their home.

A garden collage

What you need
Suitable surface for the collage to be constructed, such as a wire fence or netting, together with a considerable number of wooden clothes-pegs; pine cones; leaves.

Preparation
If using netting, make sure it is attached it to a wall securely in advance. You may also wish to add some extra items around the outdoor area in advance, such as pine cones, different leaves and so on.

What to do
Show the children an example of a collage or pictures of collages of different types. Explain to them that they are going to make a natural collage, using natural items from around the outdoor play area.

Take them outside to see what they can find, showing them how to attach each item to the fence or netting. They may be able to simply poke them in, or they may need to use the wooden clothes-pegs. Talk to the children about the items they have found and help them to decide where best to place them. Encourage them to step back and admire their work, and to modify their ideas as they go along.

Try to leave the collage outside, as decoration, if the weather is fine.

Support and extension
Show the children where best to fasten items, to avoid crushing them or damaging them in any way. Older children could be encouraged to visually divide the collage up (sorting by one feature) for example, by colour or by type (leaves, petals and so on).

Further ideas
■ Help the children to make collage cards, perhaps linked to an event such as Harvest.
■ Provide books about seasons, helping children to learn the names of various natural items.
■ Let the children paint using leaves, twigs and (washed) feathers instead of brushes for interesting effects.

Which instrument?

What you need
Copies of 'What sound?' photocopiable sheet on page 79; instruments to match the pictures (drum, tambourine, rainmaker, cabasa, maracas and bells); screen such as a large cardboard box; pebbles or small wooden bricks.

What to do
Take the children outside and ask them to collect six pebbles from around the play area. If no pebbles are available, provide small wooden bricks (place them around the area).

Sit everyone in a semi-circle in a suitable space. Each child needs to sit with their pebbles in front of them. Give each child a copy of the activity sheet and show them the instruments that match the pictures. Demonstrate the sounds the instruments make, showing them the different ways you may play each one (shake, tap, strum, pluck and so on).

Now explain to the children that each time they hear an instrument being played, they need to identify which it is and place a pebble on the corresponding picture. Use the screen to shield the instrument you are playing from the children's vision. At the end of the activity, ask the children to place their pebbles back on the garden area.

Repeat the activity regularly using different instruments each time, helping to build on the children's knowledge of instruments from around the world.

LEARNING OBJECTIVES
STEPPING STONE
Explore and learn how sounds can be changed.

EARLY LEARNING GOAL
Recognise and explore how sounds can be changed, sing simple songs from memory, recognise repeated sounds and sound patterns and match movements to music.

GROUP SIZE
Whole group.

Support and extension
Start by only using two instruments with younger children. Older children will enjoy being the person who chooses and plays the hidden instruments.

Further ideas
■ Help the children to make their own musical instruments, for example, fill margarine tubs with gravel, pebbles, twigs and so on, or bang two stones together.

■ Make a giant rainmaker with the children using a length of old garden hosepipe. Add gravel to the hosepipe, seal up each end and help the children to work co-operatively with each other to make the rain, by tipping the hosepipe gradually.

■ Give the children metal spoons or rods, and let them explore different sounds around the outdoor play area by tapping a variety of objects. Which make a sound? Which vibrate?

HOME LINKS
Encourage parents to let their children make instruments from items around the home.

Whatever the weather

LEARNING OBJECTIVES

STEPPING STONE

Explore the different sounds of instruments.

EARLY LEARNING GOAL

Recognise and explore how sounds can be changed, sing simple songs from memory, recognise repeated sounds and sound patterns and match movements to music.

GROUP SIZE

Whole group.

What you need

Range of musical instruments to represent a variety of different types of weather; sheets of cardboard; scissors.

What to do

Invite the children into the outdoor play area with you to find out what the weather is like. Play each instrument, letting the children decide which of the instruments you have chosen to use will represent the weather 'today'. What type of weather does each of the other instruments represent? For example, a tinkling bell might mean snow falling, a boom on the drum might be thunder, and a clash of the cymbals could be lightning.

Now explain to the children that you will be playing each of the instruments in turn and that you would like them to move around like the weather that each instrument represents, for example, skipping and dancing in the sun; stamping in the rainstorm and so on. Ask the children to demonstrate their own ideas and praise them for their attempts. Tell them to listen out carefully for a change in the weather. Ensure that there is plenty of space for the children to move around freely.

HOME LINKS

Encourage parents to play weather 'Who am I?' or similar games with their children. Ask the children to bring an item from home linked to the weather to show everyone. This might be a photograph taken in the snow, a sun-hat or a special umbrella.

Support and extension

Limit the number of instruments to three for younger children and suggest some movements that they might copy. Encourage older children to link their movements together in a 'weather dance'.

Further ideas

■ Play a game of weather 'Who am I?'. For example, 'I am cold, I am soft, I am white. Who am I?'.
■ Vary the game slightly by making a set of weather symbols to place around your outdoor area. When the children hear a weather sound, they must go to the correct symbol and stand there before dancing around it with their weather movements.

Changing the sounds

What you need
Empty milk bottle (or similar glass container) for each child plus one spare; one or two plant troughs (dependent on the numbers of children taking part in the activity); bowls of sand, soil and sawdust (include large spoons or scoops in each); jugs of water; wooden stick for each child.

Preparation
Position a low table or bench in a suitable place in the outdoor play area. Gather together all the items needed for the activity. Remember that the bottles should remain in the trough and that the children should be closely supervised whenever there is a glass object involved.

What to do
Invite a maximum of eight children to accompany you into the outdoor play area. Allocate each child a bottle within one of the troughs. Explain to the children that they are going to make 'music' by tapping their milk bottle with a stick, and then seeing how they can make changes to the sound it makes.

Invite each child in turn to carefully 'play' their bottle, then ask them all to make the sound together. They should all sound about the same. Next,

encourage each child to select something to add to their bottle from the bowls or jugs.

When all the children have added something to their bottles, ask them to listen as they each take turns to tap their bottles once again. Discuss with them how the sound has changed and why they each sound slightly different. Use the spare bottle to remind them how it sounded before.

Support and extension
Younger children may need adult help to add their chosen medium to their bottle. Older children can be encouraged to think of alternative mediums to add to the bottles (gravel, wood shavings and so on).

Further ideas
■ Let the children fill plastic plant pots with different mediums. How does the sound differ when these are tapped?
■ Use wooden or metal poles to make different sounds around the outside play area, for example, along fences or across gravel. Note and discuss the differences in the sounds.

LEARNING OBJECTIVES
STEPPING STONE
Explore and learn how sounds can be changed.

EARLY LEARNING GOAL
Recognise and explore how sounds can be changed, sing simple songs from memory, recognise repeated sounds and sound patterns and match movements to music.

GROUP SIZE
Six to eight children.

HOME LINKS
What sounds can the children make, and then change around their home?

The wizard's brew

LEARNING OBJECTIVES
STEPPING STONE
Use available resources to create props to support role-play.

EARLY LEARNING GOAL
Use their imagination in art and design, music, dance, imaginative and role-play and stories.

GROUP SIZE
Whole group.

What you need
Large 'pot' that can be used by the children as the wizard's cauldron; water; a garden stick; copies of 'Here we go round the wizard's brew' photocopiable sheet on page 80.

Preparation
Half fill the cauldron with cold water.

What to do
Explain to the children that they are going to make a wizard's magic brew in a big cauldron. Introduce the concept of the cauldron with a picture or a story involving witches or wizards, remembering not to make the story too scary for young children.

Explain to the children that the brew will be made by collecting items from around the outdoor play area. Give the children suggestions of what sort of things they might like to put in the cauldron, such as petals, leaves, grass, small bits of sticks and so on.

Take them outside to collect their 'potions', and demonstrate how to drop them in and stir the cauldron without spilling any water. When the magic brew is ready, all the children stand in a circle around the cauldron and one child is chosen to be the first wizard. Sing 'Here we go round the wizard's brew' to the tune of 'Here We Go Round the Mulberry Bush' as you move slowly around the cauldron!

Support and extension
Remember that three-year-old children will commonly have nightmares – so make sure that the wizards and witches that you talk about are always friendly and kind! Encourage older children to think of nice spells while they stir in their potions.

HOME LINKS
Encourage parents to read books such as *Meg and Mog* by Helen Nicoll and Jan Pienkowski (Puffin Books), or *The Worst Witch* by Jill Murphy (Puffin Books).

Further ideas
■ Let the children use blown-down sticks as broom sticks, to 'fly' around the play area.
■ Make 'wands' from discarded plant foliage (leaves from plants such as golden rod are ideal), and make 'friendly' spells.
■ Paint 'magic' signs such as stars and moons on the ground with water.

Hello scarecrow

What you need
Range of clothing suitable for a scarecrow, such as hats, shirts, waistcoats and so on (optional).

What to do
Introduce the topic of scarecrows to the children, talking about what they look like, where they are usually found and what they might be wearing.

Explain to the children that they are going to play a game in which they are pretending to cross the field with a scarecrow in. The game is called 'Hello Mr/Miss Scarecrow' (and the refrain is, 'Hello Mr/Miss Scarecrow, may we cross your field today please?').

Take the children to a spacious area outside. One child is chosen to be the scarecrow and stands in the middle of the area, while the other children stand at one side. The children call out to the scarecrow, 'Hello Mr/Miss Scarecrow, may we cross your field today please?'. The scarecrow, initially guided by the adult, says, 'Yes, when you have put on your boots/hat/ jacket,' and so on.

The children perform the requested action and then ask the question again, 'Hello Mr/ Miss Scarecrow, may we…'. The game continues until the scarecrow simply calls out, 'Yes!' and they all rush across to the other side.

The game can then start again with another child being the scarecrow.

Support and extension
Help younger children to practise the actions for putting on the imaginary items of clothing before the game begins. Older children may enjoy actually having the props to dress up in as the scarecrow calls them out.

Further ideas
■ Make a scarecrow and tie it to a post outside.
■ Make 'clackers' with sticks loosely tied together and talk about why farmers chase birds away.
■ Plant seeds in the ground and cover with lengths of string to protect the seeds from being eaten by birds.

LEARNING OBJECTIVES
STEPPING STONE
Play alongside other children who are engaged in the same theme.

EARLY LEARNING GOAL
Use their imagination in art and design, music, dance, imaginative and role-play and stories.

GROUP SIZE
Whole group.

HOME LINKS
Encourage parents to talk to their children about how they protect seeds and plants from birds, slugs, snails and frost in their garden at home.

The dragon dance

What you need
Large piece of material, such as a table-cloth, sheet or blanket that is long enough to cover all the children; felt or card; pens.

Preparation
With the children's help, add the appropriate facial features to the dragon, using circles of card or felt, and use pens to make eyes and nostrils for the front end.

What to do
Tell the children about the dragon dance – it takes place during Teng Chieh (the event which marks the end of the Chinese New Year celebrations). Lanterns are lit and carried, and the dragon dance (or lion dance) is a main part of this event.

Take the children outside and explain to them that they are going to form their own dragon dance. Explain that this will involve them moving as a group in a line, under the 'dragon' costume. Remind the children that they need to be aware of the other 'parts' of the dragon, both in front and behind them, and that they need to move in co-operation with others. Let each child take a turn in directing the path of the dragon, either by being at the head or by leading the dragon round the play area.

As they begin to walk around the outdoor play space, encourage the children to move in a range of directions and to develop sequences of movements, such as three steps forward, one step to the left, two steps to the right and so on.

Support and extension
Younger children will need some help and assistance to choose which direction the dragon will move in. Encourage older children to develop a repetitive sequence of movements.

Further ideas
■ Help the children to make Chinese lanterns to hang up or place along the ground, to indicate the route of the procession.
■ Show the children pictures of all the animals that form the sequence of the twelve year Chinese calendar and move as each animal in turn. Tell the children which 'animal year' they were born in.

In the garden I can...

What you need
Sheet of A4 paper for each child; pencils; crayons or pens; board for each child to rest on while they draw.

Preparation
Draw up to five boxes on each sheet of paper (depending on how many of the senses you will be asking the children to focus).

What to do
Remind the children of each of their senses and give them some examples of how they might use their senses in the outdoor play area. For example, hearing the wind or smelling the flowers and so on.

Invite the children to accompany you outside and ask them to draw examples of how they have used their senses. You may specify that you want a drawing for each sense, or that you would like them to choose one or two senses to focus on – for example, drawing pictures of things they have seen or heard.

Support and extension
Give younger children additional examples or prompts. Encourage older children to write (or copy) labels underneath each picture.

■■■■■■■■■■■■■■■■

Further ideas
■ Grow herbs outside and encourage the children to smell them. Include fragrant herbs, such as basil, coriander, sage, mint, lemon mint, thyme and rosemary.
■ Encourage children to gently feel the different leaves and foliage around the play area. Which feel smooth? Which feel feathery? Which feel prickly?
■ Provide a tray of garden smells for the children to identify, using scented soaps of lavender, rose petals, jasmine and lily of the valley to represent flower 'smells'.
■ Provide a feely box of garden items for the group to identify by touch. Include items such as pine cones, conkers (not in their prickly cases), a crunchy leaf, petal, acorn, twig and so on.

LEARNING OBJECTIVES
STEPPING STONE
Show an interest in what they see, hear, smell, touch and feel.

EARLY LEARNING GOAL
Respond in a variety of ways to what they see, hear, smell, touch and feel.

■■■■■■■■■■

GROUP SIZE
Whole group.

■■■■■■■■■■

HOME LINKS
Encourage parents to talk to their children at home about how they are using their senses. For example smelling their food cooking, hearing the bath running and so on.

■■■■■■■■■

Making a flower

What you need
At least one PE hoop; sunflower seed; picture of a sunflower; natural materials such as sand, gravel, fallen leaves and petals.

What to do
Show the children a sunflower seed and ask them if they know what it is. Explain that the tiny seed grows into a very large yellow flower. Show them a picture of a sunflower.

Tell the children that they are going to make a large flower design in the outdoor play area. Explain that the hoop will act as the head of the flower. Take them outside and ask them to think what they might be able to find to fill in the flower head. Suggest natural items such as petals, leaves, moss, sand, pebbles and gravel.

Encourage the children to collect items and gradually make the flower colourful. Show them how to position large leaves around the outside of the hoop to give a petal effect. If available, encourage the use of red or golden leaves.

If possible take a photograph of the flower to put on display as a permanent reminder of the activity.

Support and extension
Help younger children to position their flower 'items' within the circumference of the PE hoop. Talk to older children about what a seed needs in order for it to grow into a healthy flower.

Further ideas
■ Read books such as *Titch* by Pat Hutchins (Bodley Head) or *Billy's Sunflower* by Nicola Moon (Little Hippo, Scholastic).
■ Let the children plant sunflower seeds and watch them grow.
■ Put sunflower seeds out for the birds and talk to the children about how much the birds enjoy them.
■ Find examples of recipes or packets of cereal that contain sunflower seeds.

Minibeast hunt

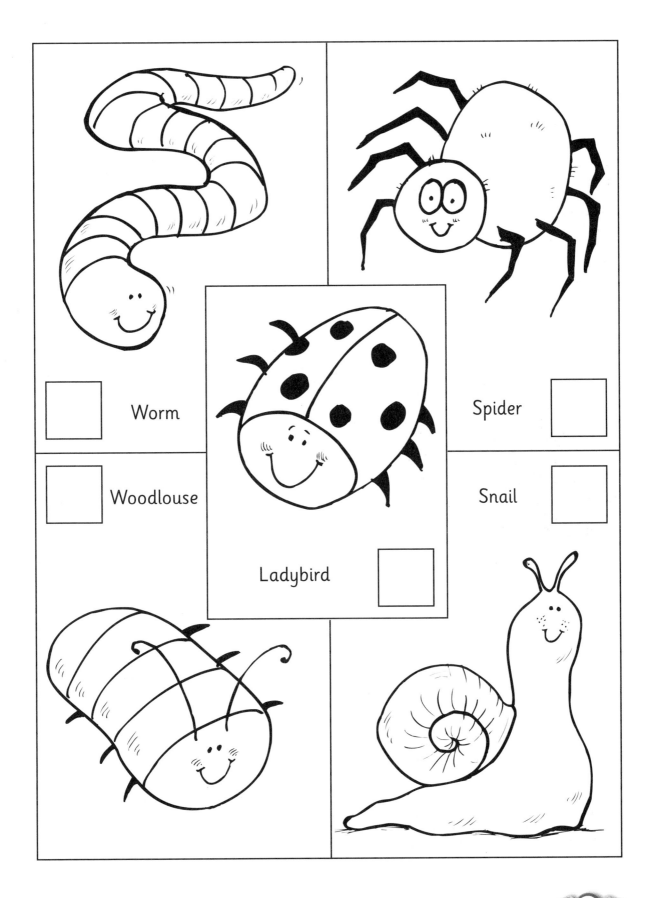

Worm ☐

Spider ☐

Woodlouse ☐

Snail ☐

Ladybird ☐

Memory game

Pot planting

You will need

What to do:

Rangoli drawings

Help the children to draw the reverse design.

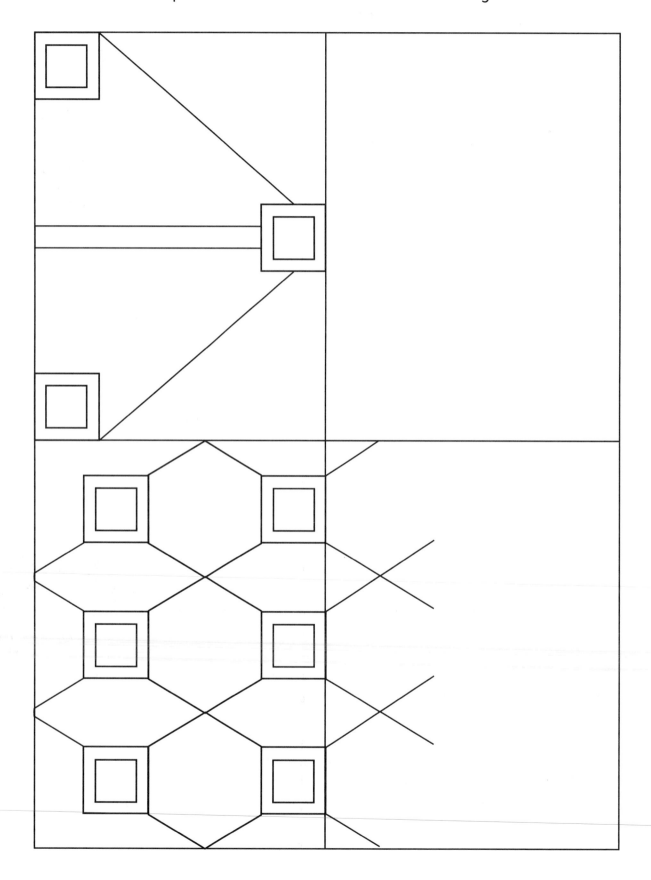

Gordon the gardener

Gordon the gardener, digging the ground
What do you think he sees?
He sees a worm, a worm, a wiggly, wiggly worm *(slithering arm actions)*

Gordon the gardener digging the ground
What do you think he sees?
He sees a snail, a snail, a slow, slimy snail
(slow hand movements, thumb tucked in to give a shell effect)

Gordon the gardener digging the ground
What do you think he sees?
He sees a spider, a spider, a tickly, tickly spider *(tickling fingers on palms)*

He sees a grasshopper, grasshopper, a hoppity, hoppity grasshopper
(hopping on spot)

He sees a caterpillar, caterpillar, a hairy, hairy caterpillar
(stroking the back of hands)

He sees a woodlouse, woodlouse, a creepy, crawly woodlouse
(fingers creeping)

He sees a bee, a bee, a busy, buzzing bee
(hands flapping fast, tucked close to the body)

He sees a fly, a fly, a flitting, flying fly
(fast, horizontal, arms-out hand movements)

He sees a ladybird, ladybird, a lovely spotty ladybird
(arm movements {as wings} above the head)

He sees a butterfly, a butterfly, a beautiful, bright butterfly
(graceful arm movements)

Gordon the gardener digging the ground
What do you think he sees?
He sees creatures, creatures, lots of lovely creatures
(children choose what they want to be, doing the appropriate actions)

Sandy Green

Five happy squirrels in a tree

(Tune: 'Five Currant Buns in a Baker's Shop')

Five happy squirrels in an old oak tree
building their winter store.
A naughty squirrel came and chased one away.
Now there are only four.

Four happy squirrels in an old oak tree
eating some acorns with glee.
A naughty squirrel came and chased one away.
Now there are only three.

Three happy squirrels in an old oak tree
hiding, and playing 'boo'.
A naughty squirrel came and chased one away.
Now there are only two.

Two happy squirrels in an old oak tree
playing, and having fun.
A naughty squirrel came and chased one away.
Now there is only one.

One happy squirrel in an old oak tree
lazing in the sun.
A naughty squirrel came and chased her/him away.
Sadly, now there are none.

Sandy Green

Name the shape

Can you join up the children to make a shape?

This is a _____
How many children are there?____

This is a _____
How many children are there?____

This is a _____
How many children are there?____

This is a _____
How many children are there?____

Identifying shapes

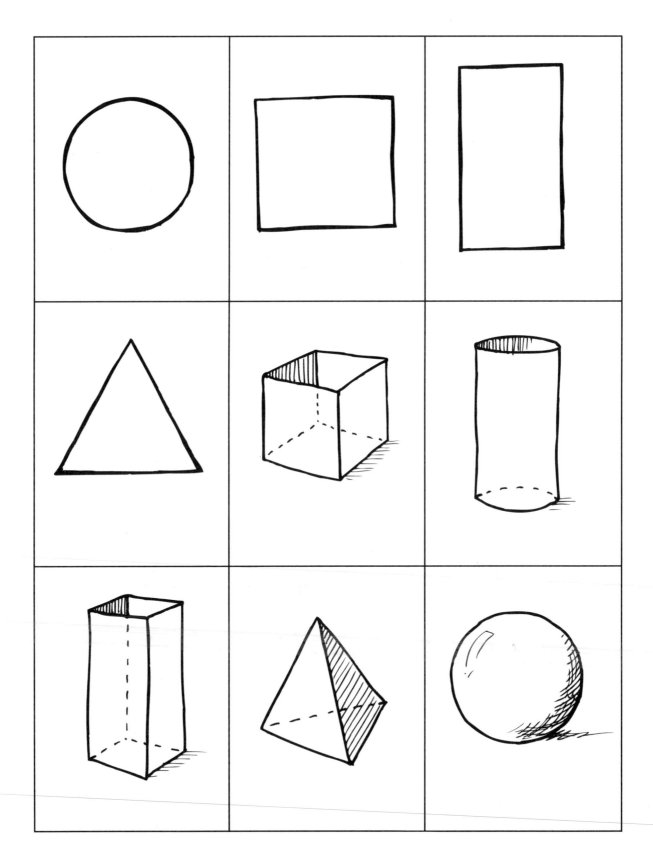

Frog fun

There was a gardener long ago

(Tune: 'There was a Princess Long Ago')

There was a gardener long ago, long ago, long ago
There was a gardener long ago long, long ago
(all children hold hands and walk in a ring)

S/he planted seeds upon the ground, upon the ground, upon the ground
S/he planted seeds upon the ground, upon the ground
(children pretend to place seeds in a line along the ground)

The rain came down and helped them grow, helped them grow, helped them grow
The rain came down and helped them grow
Helped them grow
(finger actions coming down like rain)

The sun shone down and soon they showed, soon they showed, soon they showed
The sun shone down and soon they showed
Soon they showed
(arms stretched over in a large arc for the sun)

The stalks they grew and stood so tall, stood so tall, stood so tall
The stalks they grew and stood so tall
Stood so tall
(stretching hands up as high as possible)

S/he cut them down to make the bread, to make the bread, to make the bread
S/he cut them down to make the bread
To make the bread
(pretending to cut the stalks with a 'scythe' action)

S/he ate the bread, with jam for tea, jam for tea, jam for tea
S/he ate the bread with jam for tea
Jam for tea *(pretending to eat!)*

Sandy Green

Counting the caterpillars

How many caterpillars can you count?

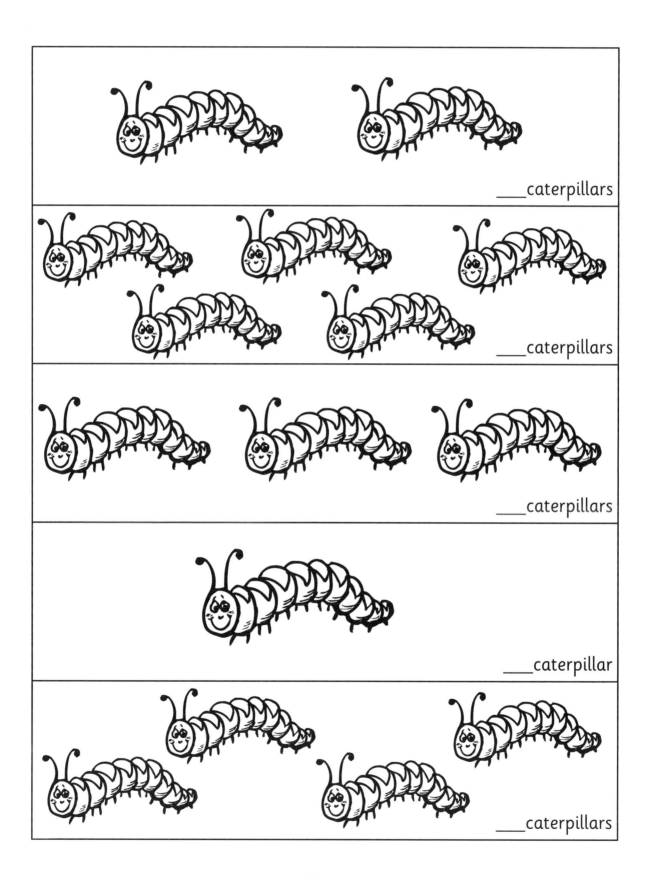

____caterpillars

____caterpillars

____caterpillars

____caterpillar

____caterpillars

Running like a racehorse

We're marching along in a line, like ants
A line, like ants, a line, like ants
We're marching along in a line, like ants
How does it make us feel?

We're jumping about like kangaroos
Like kangaroos, like kangaroos
We're jumping about like kangaroos
How does it make us feel?

We're running around like a racing horse
A racing horse, a racing horse
We're running around like a racing horse
How does it make us feel?

We're leaping across like great big lions
Great big lions, great big lions
We're leaping across like great big lions
How does it make us feel?

We're striding about like elephants huge
Elephants huge, elephants huge
We're striding about like elephants huge
How does it make us feel?

We're flying high like golden eagles
Golden eagles, golden eagles
We're flying high like golden eagles
How does it make us feel?

Sandy Green

What sound?

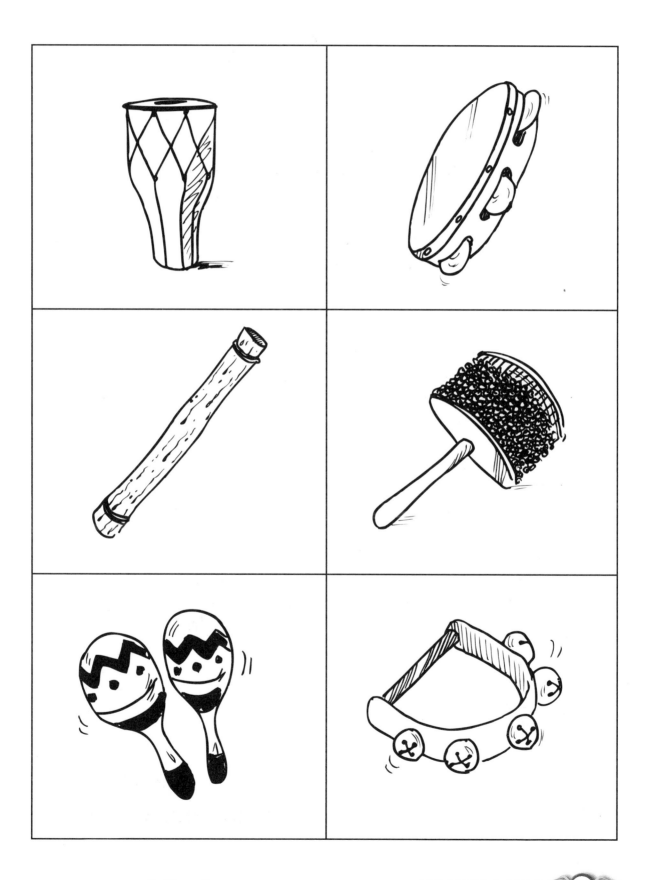

Here we go round the wizard's brew

(Tune: 'Here We Go Round the Mulberry Bush')

Here we go round the wizard's brew, the wizard's brew, the wizard's brew.
Here we go round the wizard's brew,
under the moon at night.
(all children hold hands and walk round in a ring)

The wizard arrives on his (her) magic broom, magic broom, magic broom.
The wizard arrives on his (her) magic broom,
under the moon at night.
(one child 'flies' around the outside of the circle, and 'lands' in the centre)

S/he stirs the pot to make a spell, to make a spell, to make a spell.
S/he stirs the pot to make a spell,
under the moon at night.
(all the children pretend to stir, while the 'wizard' stirs the pot)

S/he sprinkles the brew with stars so bright, starts so bright, stars so bright.
S/he sprinkles the brew with stars so bright,
under the moon at night.
(All children 'sprinkle' stars)

The magic worked and her/his friends could fly. Friends could fly, friends could fly.
The magic worked and her/his friends could fly,
under the moon at midnight.
(all the children start to 'fly')

Sandy Green